Ferenczi Revisited

Ferenczi Revisited explores Sándor Ferenczi's most significant contributions to psychoanalysis and their relevance for contemporary practice.

The book covers a range of topics, including Ferenczi's trauma theory, his technical innovations and his unique perspective on the end of analysis. Miguel Gutiérrez-Peláez also provides insight into Ferenczi's intellectual connections with figures such as Sigmund Freud, Donald Winnicott, Jacques Lacan, Jacques Derrida, and Sándor Márai, among others.

Ferenczi Revisited will be essential reading for psychoanalysts, psychologists, and psychiatrists—both professionals and students—as well as clinicians working with trauma. It will also appeal to academics and scholars of philosophy, psychoanalytic theories and techniques, the history of psychoanalysis, and the intersection of literature and psychoanalysis.

Miguel Gutiérrez-Peláez, PhD, is Full Professor in the Psychology Program at the School of Medicine and Health Sciences, Universidad del Rosario, Colombia. He is a practicing psychoanalyst in Bogotá and a member of the World Association of Psychoanalysis (AMP) and the Nueva Escuela Lacaniana (NEL).

Ferenczi Revisited

Tongues, Trauma, and Transformation

Miguel Gutiérrez-Peláez

Routledge
Taylor & Francis Group

LONDON AND NEW YORK

Designed cover image: Getty Images

First published 2026
by Routledge
4 Park Square, Milton Park, Abingdon, Oxon OX14 4RN

and by Routledge
605 Third Avenue, New York, NY 10158

*Routledge is an imprint of the Taylor & Francis Group,
an informa business*

For Product Safety Concerns and Information please contact our
EU representative GPSR@taylorandfrancis.com. Taylor & Francis
Verlag GmbH, Kaufingerstraße 24, 80331 München, Germany.

Trademark notice: Product or corporate names may be trademarks
or registered trademarks, and are used only for identification and
explanation without intent to infringe.

British Library Cataloguing-in-Publication Data
A catalogue record for this book is available from the British
Library

ISBN: 978-1-041-12158-9 (hbk)
ISBN: 978-1-041-12157-2 (pbk)
ISBN: 978-1-003-66332-4 (ebk)

DOI: 10.4324/9781003663324

Typeset in Times New Roman
by KnowledgeWorks Global Ltd.

To Josefina

Contents

Preface

The ten chapters of *Ferenczi Revisited. Tongues, Trauma, and Transformation* explore Sándor Ferenczi's most significant contributions to psychoanalysis and their relevance for contemporary practice. The book covers a range of topics, including Ferenczi's trauma theory, his technical innovations, his unique perspective on the end of analysis, and his intellectual connections with figures such as Sigmund Freud, Donald Winnicott, Jacques Lacan, Jacques Derrida, and Sándor Márai, among others.

My engagement with Ferenczi's work spans many years. Both my master's and doctoral theses were devoted to his contributions, and, over the past 20 years, I have researched and written extensively on his theories in journal articles, book chapters, and monographs. Two of my books—*Confusion of Tongues: A Return to Sándor Ferenczi* (2018) and *Sándor Ferenczi: A Contemporary Introduction* (2022, co-authored with A. Fergusson)—were published by Routledge. In addition, I have published numerous articles on Ferenczi in both English and Spanish across various academic journals. In this volume, I have compiled my most significant articles, translating those originally published in Spanish into English and revising and rewritting them for this edition. Some of the chapters appear here for the first time in publication. This volume provides a unique occasion to bring together and share my most significant contributions to the study of whom I consider one of the most impactful figures in the history of psychoanalysis.

Throughout my research, I have come to understand Ferenczi's concept of "confusion of tongues" as his attempt to grasp the traumatic dimension of language. It is his version of what Jacques Lacan would later call the Real. While this suggests that human relations are always marked by misunderstanding, it is also true that it is precisely because there is a confusion of tongues that the entire field of invention in human existence opens up. There is no translation without loss, but there is also surprise, creation, and oxymoron. This is the field of human relations—and certainly of psychoanalytic practice.

It is from this perspective that I return to Ferenczi in the pages that follow. My aim is not only to situate his ideas in their historical and clinical context, but also to show how they continue to resonate with contemporary psychoanalytic questions. The dialogue with other authors provides one path for this exploration, but above all, Ferenczi's work opens a space for thinking about trauma, language, and invention in ways that continue to shape psychoanalytic practice today.

Acknowledgements

These pages are indebted to many people—family, friends, colleagues, and teachers—who have sustained and encouraged my interest and passion for the themes explored in this book. I am grateful to Professor Alberto Fergusson, co-author of one of the chapters, with whom I have had the privilege of engaging in extensive conversations about Sándor Ferenczi and psychoanalysis throughout our years at the Center for Psychosocial Studies (CEPSO) of the Universidad del Rosario. My thanks also go to Professor Emilio Herrera, likewise co-author of one of the chapters, whose friendship has nourished both my writing and my psychoanalytic practice. I am grateful to Taylor & Francis, Routledge, *International Journal of Psychoanalysis*, *Universitas Psychologica*, *Revista Psicoanálisis*, *Affectio Societatis*, *Revista Colombiana de Psiquiatría*, *Contemporary Psychoanalysis*, and *Revista Universitaria de Psicoanálisis* for kindly granting permission to reproduce selected parts of the work included in this publication. I thank *Universidad del Rosario* and *CEPSS* for believing in this project. To Susannah Frearson of Routledge, for her kindness and for embracing the idea of this book with enthusiasm, as well as to the entire Routledge editorial and publishing team for their support. To Verónica, Rodrigo, and Rafael, for their love and wisdom. To Josefina Dartiguelongue, for her profound friendship and for having been an indispensable interlocutor in the shaping of the ideas contained in this book. And finally, to those who have whispered the quiet reminder "Cultivate your garden": a true Thalassal embrace.

Chapter 1

Sándor Ferenczi and Donald W. Winnicott

Trauma, Environment, and Technique[1]

Miguel Gutiérrez-Peláez and Emilio Herrera-Pardo

Winnicott Citing Ferenczi

It is difficult to accurately assess the effect Sándor Ferenczi's work had on the clinical and theoretical production of Donald W. Winnicott. From his writings, we know that he cited him on two occasions. These references indicate that Winnicott had access to Ferenczi's work and not only through Melanie Klein's use thereof. It is not probable that any formal meetings took place between the two psychoanalysts. Winnicott completed his training as an adult analyst in 1934, a year after the death of Sándor Ferenczi. In his work "Classification: is there a psychoanalytic contribution to psychiatric classification?", read at a scientific conference held by the British Psycho-Analytical Society on 18 March 1959, Winnicott (1959) states that

> gradually and in the course of time, the study of psychosis began to make more sense. Ferenczi (1931) contributed significantly by looking at a failed analysis of a patient with character disorder, not simply as a failure of selection but as a deficiency of psycho-analytic technique. The idea implied here was that psycho-analysis could learn to adapt its technique to the character disorder or the borderline case without turning over into management, and indeed without losing the label psycho-analysis. Eventually Melanie Klein (1932, 1948) made her specific contributions showing that in the analysis of children psychotic disorders must be encountered, and that these could be dealt with if met by adequate technique, so that failure to deal with psychotic manifestations in childhood meant for her (as for Ferenczi) a failure of technique, not a failure of selection.
>
> (p. 151).

It is interesting that he references Ferenczi's 1931 work in this citation (written in 1931 and presented in 1932 at the Wiesbaden Congress), as it was specifically "Confusion of Tongues between Adults and the Child" that marked the turning point in Freud and Ferenczi's relationship, which once again postulated the effective reality of trauma, a theme that Freud assumed was overcome based on the notion of "psychic reality" (for more on this matter, see Masson, Rachman, Sylwan, Hidas, and Gutiérrez-Peláez, 2009, pp. 3–7). Moreover, it is worth noting the fact

DOI: 10.4324/9781003663324-1

that Winnicott underlines the importance Ferenczi gives to the necessity of adapting the environment to the patient's needs. Ferenczi had worked on this a few years earlier, in 1927, in "The Adaptation of the Family to the Child" (1984e).

Winnicott's (1958) other and final reference to Ferenczi appeared one year earlier, in "Ernest Jones", which was published in the *International Journal of Psychoanalysis*. Borgogno (2008) has highlighted several similarities between Ferenczi and Winnicott, referring to the relationship between their works and the psychoanalytic community. Ferenczi was subjected to direct censorship, and it was not until 1949 that his work began to circulate, almost coinciding with that of Winnicott. Although the British author did not undergo explicit censorship, Borgogno does note that Winnicott felt he had not been sufficiently recognized by his peers. That said, when Ferenczi's works were published, which coincided in time with Winnicott's writings, a particular interest in the subject of countertransference can be found in both theoretical bodies. For both authors, the emotional response of the therapist is fundamental to the technique and analytical process. Borgogno also underlines the fact that both authors explain antisocial behaviour on the basis of childhood neglect.

The Role of the Environment

The importance of the role the environment plays on mental health is more than evident in Winnicott's theoretical developments, and he is undoubtedly the most noteworthy point of reference in this regard, with his concepts of active adaptation, the facilitating environment, and the good-enough mother. With this in mind, his concepts resonate in various passages of Ferenczi's *Clinical Diary* (1932), such as, for example, in the following paragraph:

> More proof that the lasting effect of the trauma stems from the absence of a kind, understanding, and enlightening environment [...] The childish personality, as yet barely consolidated, does not have the capacity to exist, so to speak, without being supported on all sides by the environment. Without this support, the psychic and organic component mechanisms diverge, explode, as it were; as yet, there is no ego-center strong enough to be worth mentioning, which could hold the whole of it together, also on its own. Children have no ego yet, but only an id; the id still reacts alloplastically, not motorically. The analysis should be able to provide for the patient the previously missing favorable milieu for building up the ego, and so put an end to that state of mimetism, which, like a conditioned reflex, only drives the person toward repetition. A new couvade, so to speak, and a new taking flight.

> (p. 289)

In his essay "Fear of Breakdown", Winnicott (1963) develops his theory that "clinical fear of breakdown is the fear of a breakdown that has already been experienced" (p. 115). The event remains rooted in a rather unique unconscious, of which he states that in this context, "unconscious means that the ego integration is not able to encompass something. The ego is too immature to gather all the phenomena into the area of personal omnipotence" (p. 115). Thus, the patient cannot recall something that is yet to occur but must experience it for the first time in transference. Regarding this point, a link can be made with Ferenczi's line of thought, who also dealt extensively with trauma. With respect to treating his traumatized patients, Ferenczi highlighted the importance of connecting with the traumatic material, which initially is only accessible through repetition, given that it only exists as an event. However, it is possible to relive it through analysis and to make an experience of it, which results in the union of the patient's fragmented personality.

Moreover, Ferenczi notes that impressions from traumatic experiences are not recorded in any psychic instance. In this sense, one might assume that no record remains precisely because of the prematurity of the trauma (and the ego), as there is no established or differentiated ego to undergo the traumatic experience, but that this experience is only accessible by reliving the trauma under the favourable therapeutic conditions afforded by the psychoanalytic treatment and with an ego that is able to make an experience of it. In his diary, Ferenczi expresses this as follows: "The analyst is able, for the first time, to link emotions with the above primal event and thus endow that event with the feeling of a real experience" (p. 38) and, later, "… for the first time a conscious experiencing-to-the-end?" (p. 157).

Deeper into the Psychology of Trauma

Dupont (1998), like Genovés (in Jiménez Avello, 1998), also argues that trauma cannot be remembered, given that it was never experienced consciously. In his diary, Ferenczi states,

> [At] the moment of the attack all illusion is destroyed, the sudden insight into this terrifying existence in the power of a madman cannot be accepted, and the state of being split that has existed up to now gives way to a state of complete dissolution. After that has run its course, as when fireworks have burnt themselves out, the entire sector of this experience disintegrates into a mass of atomized debris.
>
> (p. 82)

Traumatic situations and their persistence, whether incestuous seductions, passionate punishments, or the terrorism of suffering (*Erschütterung*), cause the split to intensify and multiply, which in turn leads the psyche to disintegrate.

For Ferenczi, psychic paralysis has to do with the interruption of the senses, the unresisting acceptance of any mechanical or psychic impression, without any mnemic trace of said impressions, even unconsciously. It is thus in no way possible that they will become accessible to memory. For this reason, the analytic situation requires conditions to be provided so that the patient may perceive his/her trauma for the first time, to which the detached feelings behind the psychic fragmentation are tied.

> In the transference the opportunity would present itself to provide that protection and support which were absent during the trauma. The love and strength of the analyst, assuming that trust in him goes deep enough and is great enough, have nearly the same effect as the embrace of a loving mother and a protective father.
>
> (p. 106)

As regards the technical innovations of both authors, this is probably Ferenczi's most controversial point and the one that led Ernest Jones (1953) to tarnish his work as psychopathological in his biography of Freud. Ferenczi worked on three different technical innovations in the last years of his life: the active technique, the relaxation and neocatharsis technique, and mutual analysis. But beyond agreeing or disagreeing with these technical innovations, criticizing their boldness or reading them as errors or excesses in the technique, they show Ferenczi's psychoanalytic passion and reveal the need to institute changes in the classical analytic technique for the treatment of certain patients.

The Need to Apply Technical Innovations

Winnicott (1955–1956), in "Clinical Varieties of Transference", reports how psychoanalysis has been applied to "well-chosen" cases of neurosis, i.e., to patients that have had "good-enough infant care", where the stages preceding the establishment of the ego are taken for granted, and it is precisely this good-enough adaptation that has allowed the ego to come into being. Thus, Winnicott emphasizes the need to bring about change in the approach to other patients besides said "well-chosen" neurotic subjects, i.e., borderline disorders, psychosis, and psychotic episodes suffered by neurotic and normal patients. Indeed, the technique Winnicott used to approach his cases is well-known, and debates have been sustained on the topic. The freedom and genuineness with which he responded to his patients in conditions that were somewhat unusual for the psychoanalytic community led him to see other kinds of patients and in different clinical situations. This also placed him under scrutiny by the psychoanalytic community. Both his book *Therapeutic consultations in child psychiatry* (1971a) and his famous *The Piggle: An Account of the Psychoanalytic Treatment of a Little Girl* (1977) are examples of Winnicott's broad clinical and technical range. His unique hospital sessions, interviews, and written communications to parents, the frequency and duration of his sessions, and his famous "psychoanalysis on demand" and "phases of intensive treatment" were some of his innovations on the traditional psychoanalytic technique. That said, none of them was an innovation that sought to establish itself as a good practice protocol, but they all saw sense in the transferential relationship with the patient and the search for a specific and singular technique so that each case could be directed towards a possible cure.

Below is an extract from the prologue of *The Piggle: An Account of the Psychoanalytic Treatment of a Little Girl*, written by Ishak Ramzy in 1974, in which he describes how in a psychoanalytic event the "psychoanalysis on demand" technique was received and debated:

> One issue in the subsequent discussion centered on the subject of whether the type of treatment Winnicott described and called 'psychoanalysis on demand' with its infrequent and irregular sessions was analysis or psychotherapy. Winnicott replied by directing attention to what he did with the transference and the unconscious, not to [...] the frequency or regularity of the analytic sessions. In the course of this discussion, an impatient listener was heard to say in an audible whisper: 'If there is any question that this is an analysis, how is it that the case of Little Hans is still considered one of the classics in psychoanalytic literature?'
>
> (p. 17)

Borgogno (2008) refers to the fact that both Ferenczi and Winnicott focus their theoretical and technical attention on the role of the mother. This interest led them, in turn, to work not only on the theoretical child but also on the real child. To consider the importance of the technique, where the analyst must not only position himself and perform the benevolent role of the mother but also receive the projections of the inadequate protector. Accordingly, both the mother and the analyst must be able to receive the baby and the patient as they are, without asking them to adapt to a particular ideal or therapy. They must be able to receive the patient-baby with his/her immature side and not push him/her towards a "somersault of adaptation". During the analysis, the patient is equipped to reproduce his/her unresolved conflict and, having contained it, to be able to transform it. This fact led Winnicott and Ferenczi to think about technique and theory differently from other psychoanalysts, including those who worked with children. Both proposed, at different points in history, the fact that, like the mother, the analyst must be able to adapt to the patient/baby and not expect adaptation from the other. However, this transformation not only arises from an internal interest, as Borgogno indicates, but also due to their clinical activities with borderline or "very disturbed" patients. Thinking about the therapist—and the mother—as the person who adapts to the patient—baby— and not vice versa carries with it a profound change in technique. Both frame and interpretation find another use and another orientation. For example, as well as being something that stems from the knowledge of the therapist, the interpretation is something that the patient creates and encounters in therapy.

Over the analyst's knowledge, what takes precedence is the genuineness of the patient (and the analyst). Borgogno indicates that for both Ferenczi and Winnicott, the mother must have a particular mental state. In Winnicott's words, she must have a "primary maternal preoccupation" and, according to Ferenczi, should consent to being "temporarily parasited". If this is not the case, the child will have to overadapt to the mother, moving away from its sense of feeling real in the world. Concepts such as "spoilt children", "wise baby", and the "false self" arise on the basis of this concept. It is thus possible to see how, for both psychoanalysts, the psychic state of the mother is fundamental in developing the subject's sense of existence and how, when this is not guaranteed, the child tends to overadapt or progress in this development (a leap into the void). Both Winnicott and Ferenczi suggest an animated, interested analyst capable of being used by the patient and who is firm but also flexible enough to adapt to the needs demanded by the analysand's inner child. In connection with the foregoing, Borgogno explores a technical similarity of the two authors, derived from the practice that prompts the consultation of borderline patients. Borgogno shows how working with patients presenting a dissociation between mind and body led Ferenczi and Winnicott to undergo a learning process and a change in their technique. In this sense, both authors:

> have in mind and share the idea that psychoanalysis is an instrument that cannot function independently or thus do without the resources and limitations of the person conducting and carrying it forward, and of the interpsychic encounter that takes place between the two members of the 'working team' (Ferenczi, 1912). Consequently, for them, the contribution of the analyst to the analysis and the desired mutative success is essential and the latter cannot be reduced in any way to a mere transmission of words and thinking contents, but *in primis* implies having to emotionally undergo the patient's painful experience and to be able to feel it, gradually coming up with an alternative solution to the one the patient has found up until that moment in his/her life.
>
> (p. 213)

We can see then that both Winnicott and Ferenczi attribute fundamental importance to the presence and role of the analyst, an analyst who not only works on the basis of knowledge but also connects to the emotional experience that an analysis implies. In his work on "the use of an object" (made up of several essays, the one used most frequently for this research was "The Use of an Object and Relating through Identifications," which consists of a presentation given at a conference in 1968, published in the *International Journal of Psycho-Analysis* in 1969, and in his book *Playing and Reality* in 1971b; this piece of work used a collection of said articles on the use of an object, presented in the book *Psycho-analytic Explorations I* in 1989), Winnicott noted that the analyst must first endure being a subjective object, but must also recognize that he or she must survive destruction and be able to position him or herself in a place that is not only the projection of the patient, but which is an object in itself, that may be used and related to.

The analyst has a body and is not merely a projection of the patient's past figures; their presence implies something. As such, the analyst must enable the paradox in which the patient creates the object (subjective object), but where the object is already there waiting to be created. The subject may relate to the other, no longer as a part or projection of themselves, but as a separate entity. But to do this, it is imperative that the analyst, like the object, survives the destruction. Thus, the changes that arise in the analysis stem from the survival of the analyst more than that of the interpretations, and this is a fundamental aspect of Winnicott's technique. Although, as we have noted, Winnicott had no influence on Ferenczi's work and the British author only makes limited references to the Hungarian, they do have one thing in common: the need for a change in technique where the patient does not adapt to the frame, but rather the frame accommodates the need of the patient, in a reconstruction, so to speak, of the child's need where the environment and the object are the ones that adapt. For example, we find the importance that empathy and intuition take for Winnicott in the role of the analyst. He considers it to be extremely important that the therapist begins not from prior and disingenuous knowledge of the patient but receives him/her from a not-knowing perspective (Gutiérrez-Peláez, 2021), from a position where the therapist's intellect is not imposed on the patient.

Similarly, it is essential to think about the concept of a good-enough mother in order to understand the role of the analyst. The latter must be good enough to adapt to the patient's needs, including the necessity of frustration, to thus be able to grow. He/she is not an analyst who relies on extensive external knowledge that proves him/her to be totally good: like the mother, who starts with no external knowledge of how to be a mother, the therapist must, as mentioned, start with his/her feelings and even have the capacity to make mistakes. Accordingly, the patient, as the baby, does not adapt to the adult; however, the mother and analyst are the ones who adjust to receive the former. Ferenczi forcefully referred to this point in his article "The Adaptation of the Family to the Child" (1984e).

Both authors draw on the idea that, due to a trauma or an environmental failure, the subject cannot continue his/her normal development and has to overadapt, thereby moving backwards as well as forwards (advancing beyond his/her developmental stage, among other things). The analysis allows for the reproduction of this traumatic moment (Gutiérrez-Peláez, 2009) in transference and enables development to be reinstated. It is a fact that both analysts worked with borderline and psychotic patients and that the emergence of this approach shaped their technical innovations and the need to introduce them into the analytic process. Winnicott, in *Playing and Reality*, understands psychoanalysis as a specialized form of playing through which communication with the self and others is achieved:

> Psychotherapy takes place in the overlap of two areas of playing, that of the patient and that of the therapist. Psychotherapy has to do with two people playing together. The corollary of this is that where playing is not possible, then the work done by the therapist is directed towards bringing the patient from a state of not being able to play into a state of being able to play.
>
> (p. 61).

The therapist not only seeks to interpret the contents of the game (or verbal content), but the environment of growth and therapy permitted by the game and analysis is also taken into account. In this sense, playing is sanity. The significant moment of the therapy "is that at which the child surprises himself or herself. It is not the moment of my clever interpretation that is significant" (p. 76).

That said, the interpretation is not rejected in itself, but it is thought that if the interpretation takes place outside the space of the therapist-analyst game, this generates confusion and is unhelpful. Even Winnicott, in his 1968 work, "The Use of an Object and Relating through Identifications", questions himself regarding his use of interpretation, reinventing his own technique:

> It appeals me to think how much deep change I have prevented or delayed in patients in a certain classification category by my personal need to interpret. If only we can wait, the patient arrives at understanding creatively and with immense joy, and I now enjoy this joy more than I used to enjoy the sense of having been clever.
>
> (p. 263)

But if the game is spontaneous, the interpretation will have therapeutic effects. In this way, the patient feels that he finds and constructs the interpretation himself, even if it comes from another.

Both Winnicott, in Playing and Reality, and Ferenczi, in his Clinical Diary, on referring to the technical elements of psychotherapy, highlight an aspect of great importance, namely, trust. Both authors link it to understanding psychoanalysis as a search for oneself. With regard to a cure, Winnicott associates trust with the patient's capacity to create, as well as with the discovery of a sense of self.

> The patient has been unable to rest because of a failure of the environmental provision, which undid the sense of trust. The therapist has, without knowing it, abandoned the professional role, and has done so by bending over backwards to be a clever analyst, and to see order in chaos.
>
> (p. 82)

Winnicott can be seen as drawing on the notion of "relaxation", made prominent by Ferenczi in his article *Relaxation and Neocatharsis* (1929b), a key text in the development of Ferenczi's own technical innovations. This concept would also serve as a precursor to the technical contributions of subsequent generations of analysts.

Final Thoughts on the Ferenczi-Winnicott Link

As Borgogno highlights, "we should not be surprised in the least then if both Ferenczi and Winnicott have been *enfants terribles* in our discipline; in many respects, they were ahead of their time" (p. 213). According to Balint, who is cited by Dupont, the disagreement between Freud and Ferenczi caused real trauma for the analytic community. "The impact of this event was so painful that the first reaction of the analytic movement was denial and silence". For Dupont,

> the analytic world reacted to the trauma by forgetting Ferenczi and his work. That said, his work has never been fully discarded, and although it is still somewhat uncomfortable, can never not be taken into account in the development of psychoanalysis. A scarcely cited but very used work, it has been rediscovered [...] We might perhaps be able to see a sort of therapeutic regression by the analytic community to the original trauma.
>
> (p. 23)

It is possible to see how, as in Freud's trauma theory, in which a second time is needed in order to give new meaning to a previous experience that resulted in trauma, Winnicott's work may have allowed an introduction to that of Ferenczi, as a spokesperson and articulator, who remained silenced for decades. Such is not the case with Ferenczi's work today—nearly a century after his death, it is currently the subject of extensive academic debate, conferences, and publications. This ongoing engagement ensures its continued relevance in contemporary psychoanalytic debates and in addressing the particularities of 21st-century psychoanalytic practice. We can salvage from it, as with Winnicott's work, one of the greatest teachings of our era: it is not the patient who adapts to the therapist's technique, but the analyst's technique works on the principle of adjusting to the particularities of the patient.

Note

1 A first version of this article published in: Gutiérrez-Peláez, M. & Herrera-Pardo, E. (2017). Environment, trauma and technical innovations: Three links between Donald W. Winnicott and Sándor Ferenczi. *Revista Colombiana de Psiquiatría, 46*(2), 121–126. http://dx.doi.org/10.1016/j.rcp.2015.12.001

Chapter 2

Sándor Ferenczi and Jacques Lacan

On the Trauma of Language[1]

Speech is telling the story of the trauma.

— Sándor Ferenczi, *Clinical Diary*
(1932, in Dupont [1988])

Ferenczian Innovations in the Treatment of Trauma

Ferenczi's 1930s trauma theory can be read either as a regressive return to the first Freudian seduction theory or as a progressive anticipation of contemporary psychoanalysis and of the deepest implications of Freudian thought. I firmly endorse the latter. Ferenczi's later writings display a complex concept of trauma that is, by no means, a return to Freud's first trauma theory, but rather the elaboration of a new psychoanalytic theory. Reading texts such as "Confusion of Tongues between the Adult and the Child" (1932/1955), Clinical Diary (1932; see Dupont, 1988), and "Notes and Fragments" (1930–1932/1955) as a return to Freud's early trauma theory has led to limited and misguided interpretations.

The Freud-Ferenczi polemic, which followed the presentation of "Confusion of Tongues between the Adult and the Child," has been thoroughly analyzed and commented upon using novel and complex historical, psychoanalytic, and psychological approaches (Berman, 1995; Blum, 1994; Gutiérrez-Peláez, 2009; Harris & Aron, 1997; Hunyady, 2012; Jones, 1953; Masson, 1984; Modell, 1991; Press, 2006; Rachman, 1989, 1997; Sabourin, 1984; Sulloway, 1979; Zaslow, 1988). The Freud-Ferenczi correspondence of those tumultuous years includes intimate and personal exchanges (Falzeder & Brabant, 2000), many of which can be linked to the issue of the Ferenczian return to the first Freudian trauma theory.

Ferenczi and Freud frequently discussed trauma theory, and Freud believed Ferenczi was reviving a theory he had left behind. Ferenczi's "Confusion of Tongues" was badly received by the psychoanalytic community (Masson, 1984, p. 151) and contributed to the forgetting and isolation of his work for many years.

DOI: 10.4324/9781003663324-2

Another quarrel between Freud and Ferenczi concerned the death drive. As I have commented elsewhere,

> ... there is indeed a less noticed aspect of the Freud-Ferenczi polemic about the Confusion of Tongues, which has to do with the drive element, and which could be expressed as follows: Whereas for Freud there is a deadly component in every subject, for Ferenczi this component is attributable to the "other"; it comes about owing to the traumatic effect of the other's action, and if this were not the case there would, in his view, be no reason for it to be unleashed.
>
> (Gutiérrez-Peláez, 2009, p. 1225)

Ferenczi refers widely to (an)other who traumatizes through abandonment, rage, and sexual abuse (Ferenczi, 1929/1955a). These are concrete actions that exceed the capacity of the child's psyche to process them in his or her framework of experience; they cannot be symbolized by the child. This forms a traumatic nucleus that shapes the symptoms and the *Wiederholungszwang*, the compulsion to repetition.[2]

As will be argued in this chapter, it is possible to read in Ferenczi's later writings a fundamental divergence from Freud's theories, producing an original and powerful trauma theory with important consequences for clinical practice.

The Traumatic Dimension of Language

A close reading of Ferenczi's later writings from 1930–1932 (Ferenczi, 1955b, 1955c, 1955d) reveals a particularly unique aspect of his trauma theory, which we could call the traumatic dimension of language. This focus on language is rarely mentioned in the psychoanalytic literature. Yet, it involves one of Ferenczi's greatest insights for contemporary psychoanalysis and is precisely the point where the work of Sándor Ferenczi and the French psychoanalyst Jacques Lacan meet. Ferenczi's theory on the relationship between trauma and language, and the effects it has on the subject, anticipates Lacan's work on the traumatic dimension of language, a dimension found in Lacan's (1997, 2007) concept of *lalangue*, to which we will return later.

Lacan admired and identified with Ferenczi for having been "excomulgated"[3] (as he called himself; see Lacan, 1998) from the IPA. As he stated in his 1953 seminar:

> Ferenczi was to some extent considered, up to 1930, to be the enfant terrible of psychoanalysis. In relation to the analytic group in general, he remained a free-wheeler. His way of raising questions showed no concern for couching itself in a manner which was, at that time, already orthodox.
>
> (Lacan, 1975, p. 208)

In Lacan's "Rome Discourse," he said that "psychoanalysts who are also mothers, even those who give our loftiest deliberations a matriarchal air, are not exempt from that confusion of tongues by which Ferenczi designated the law of the relationship between the child and the adult" (Lacan, 2006a, p. 36, cited by Barzilai, 1997, p. 568). Barzilai also cites Lacan's "... further praises [for] Ferenczi for posing 'the question of the analyst's being ... very early in the history of analysis,' and thereby introducing 'the problem of analytic action' almost 50 years before in an essay entitled 'Introjection and Transference'"(1909). According to Lacan, the essay "anticipated by a long way all the themes later developed about this topic" (Lacan, 2002 p. 250, cited by Barzilai, 1997, p. 568). Of course, there are other times in Lacan's seminars and writings in which he speaks poorly of some of Ferenczi's theoretical developments, such as when he states, in relation to the further expansions of this work by his Hungarian disciples, that they are now dispersed and will soon be turned into ashes (Lacan, 1958/2002, p. 33). As Barzilai (1997) puts it:

> ... clearly, he [Lacan] admires the risk-taking methods and intellectual enterprise of Ferenczi. He likes him whom he is like. Lacan has read the work of Ferenczi with considerable attention and admiration. However, he also charges him with expounding a doctrine of developmental stages for which Ferenczi was not solely responsible, while ignoring or "forgetting" to mention his insight into the cognitive gains of ambivalence—an insight that predates Lacan's thesis about the dialectical structure of human thought.
>
> (p. 568)[4]

The concept of lalangue, a particularly "dark" concept in Lacan's work (beyond the evident complexity of his writings), could be related to the difficulty of using language to talk about that which cannot be grasped by the contours of language; taking hold of the limits of language and symbolization through a symbolic medium such as language. Evans (1996) states that

> Lacan coins the term lalangue (from the definite article la and the noun langue) to refer to those noncommunicative aspects of language which, by playing on ambiguity and homophony, give rise to a kind of jouissance[5] (S 20, p. 126). The term 'language' now becomes opposed to lalangue.
>
> (p. 100)

So, whereas language is the cultural heritage of the Other[6] and is directed to the other, lalangue is absolutely singular, private, and does not address the Other.

> Lalangue is the primary chaotic substrate of polysemy out of which language is constructed, almost as if language is some ordered superstructure sitting on top of this substrate: 'language is with no doubt made of lalangue. It is an elucubration of knowledge [savoir] about lalangue' (S20, p. 127).
>
> (p. 100)

It is important, however, not to confuse this elaboration of a superstructure with a metalanguage. Rather, instead of lalangue "completing" language, it is the fair proof of the "inconsistency" of language. Lalangue is not a formal or communicative medium, like the language of linguistics, but rather an experience (Toboul, 2005, p. 78). The child's lalangue is grounded in the physical/sensual experience of the infant engrossed in the sensual production of sound, and in free expression of "itself," in the absence of an Other. This babbling (or chirping) is not directed to an Other; it lies in a private experience that mobilizes a jouissance.

It is commonly accepted that what is traumatic is that which cannot be symbolized, that is, the experience of the real that does not enter into the symbolic order. But what if there is an original (failed)[7] rejection (Freud used the word *Ausstossung* [expulsion] as opposed to *Bejahung* [affirmation]) of the symbolic order in the infant? What if language itself constitutes the *Urtrauma* (that "pre-primal-trauma [*ururtraumatischen*]" (Ferenczi, 1932b, p. 83)? That portion of the child's language (babbling), which is not directed to the other, is the trace (mark) of the original enjoyment, before language disrupts it to establish order, a symbolic order. Precisely, the substance of lalangue is extracted from the child's glossolalia (Toboul, 2005, p. 58) or babbling. In an entry entitled "The Language of the Unconscious," Ferenczi (1939/1955b) writes:

If the intellectual cs [conscious] urge to communicate is completely eliminated and the speech organs are given free reign… there comes—after senseless vowels and consonants (as in the play of infants with lips and tongue) imitations of things, animals, and people.

(p. 265)

Ferenczi intends to unveil a realm before language, free of trauma; concepts such as "Thálassa," the primordial sea, or "infant," he who is speechless or unable to speak, point directly to this. In *Thalassa: A Theory of Genitality* (1924/1968), Ferenczi establishes precise analogies between sleep and regression to primordial states of the organic, past the womb, to the poikilothermia[8] of diverse amphibians and fishes (p. 76). More radically, as Ferenczi structures the basis of his bioanalysis,[9] he states that:

By carrying over into biology this piece of insight gained in the psychic sphere, it is possible for us to think of coitus and sleep as the conducting off of current traumatic stimuli and, at the same time, the expression of the striving to reproduce the intrauterine and thalassal situation seemingly long since transcended— nay, we could even perceive in them a return to still more archaic and primitive strivings toward repose (impulse towards the inorganic state, death impulse).

(Ferenczi, 1924/1968, p. 85)

The relation between sleep and regression, in reference to trauma, is also displayed in the *Clinical Diary* (1932; see Dupont, 1988), where he writes: "Sleep is regression to a primordial unity, as yet unsplit. (Without consciousness and, when completely without objects, dreamless.) Regression to the pretraumatic" (p. 113).

The case of B. in Ferenczi's *Clinical Diary* (1932; see Dupont, 1988) illustrates this traumatic dimension of language.

> Throughout the day's activities, which consist of tasks that, though very unpleasant, must be performed, there is a soft humming of a few melodies [p. 17]. … incessant melodies were going on [p. 20]. For years, as a child, she could not fall asleep without first crouching and banging her head, always the forehead, against the mattress, over and over again with considerable force. She had to give up this procedure as she grew up, but appears to have invented analogous but less obvious substitutes: endlessly repeated melodies; an endlessly sustained long note that occasionally shifts to a higher tone, then after a while rises higher and higher, but so that the change occurs in jerks or waves.
>
> (pp. 22–23)

Nevertheless, "melody" implies a symbolic organization that is nonexistent in lalangue. In the entry of July 19, Ferenczi writes: "… in addition to her clearly conscious work of thinking [*Denkarbeit*] she also has a melody permanently in her head, in fact a disharmonious polyphony, which she must resolve by musically logical means" (p. 162). In the vignettes of B., there is no reference to a communicative intention in her vocal sounds; the patient uses these melodies, apparently, along the lines of the pure jouissance of this frivolous sounding.

Regarding how exclamations are produced with sounds that do not belong to a particular native language, Heller-Roazen (2008) writes:

> Nowhere is language more "itself" than at the moment it seems to leave the terrain of its sound and sense, assuming the sound shape of what does not—or cannot—have a language of its own: animal sounds, natural, or mechanical noises. It is here that one language, gesturing beyond itself in a speech that is none, opens itself to the nonlanguage that precedes it and that follows it. It is here, in the utterance of the strange sounds that the speakers of a tongue thought themselves incapable of making, that a language shows itself as an "exclamation" in the literal sense of the term: a "calling out" (*ex-clamare*, *Aus-ruf*), beyond or before itself, in the sounds of the inhuman speech it can neither completely recall nor fully forget.
>
> (p. 18)

Language is traumatic in various ways. Words can hurt, degrade, conjure, and produce anxiety. Words can be unforgettable; they determine destinies. Words can take hold of the body, mark it, and transform it, as hysterics have taught us. Language is also traumatic through the lalangue it carries, those noncommunicative aspects of language, a private tongue mobilizing a form of jouissance that can produce an unpleasant satisfaction for it lays beyond the Freudian pleasure principle.

Finally, language is traumatic because it definitively transforms an infant's relation to the world, leaving only subtle traces of what that relation before language could have been.

Ferenczi-Lacan and the Real

Lacan (1974–1975) divides reality into three different orders (RSI): the Imaginary order, which consists of our fantasies; the Symbolic order, which includes all the different dimensions of language and communication; and the Real, an order that is neither accessible to language nor to fantasy, but which touches and haunts both. According to Shepherdson (2008):

> The real is... an effect of symbolization, and thus an abyss in the field of meaning, a product of the Other, in Lacan's language; consequently, it does not have the status of a natural entity... but is rather a void introduced into being by the operation of representation. (p. 94);... the real is a dimension of immediate existence or prediscursive reality that is never actually available to us as such, but only appears through the intervention of the imaginary or the symbolic [order].
>
> (p. 30)

The RSI are not independent but entangled, constricted in what Lacan called the "Borromean knot."[10] This knotting of the imaginary, the symbolic, and the real can be illustrated through the myth of the Medusa's or Gorgon's face. Italian philosopher Giorgio Agamben (1999) refers to the Gorgon's face as that which cannot be represented (the Medusa's face cannot be seen without being turned into stone). However, paradoxically, all of the representations that exist of the Medusa (Cellini, Rubens, Caravaggio, Bernini, Böcklin, even ancient ones, such as those of the Basilica Cistern, the Temple of Artemis, and the Rondanini Medusa, amongst many others) are precisely of her face.

First, the Gorgon does not have a face in the sense expressed by the Greek term prosopon, which etymologically signifies "what stands before the eyes, what gives itself to be seen." The prohibited face, which cannot be seen because it produces death, is for the Greeks a nonface, and as such is never designated by prosopon. Yet for the Greeks, this impossible vision is, at the same time, absolutely inevitable. Not only is the Gorgon's nonface represented innumerable times in sculpture and vase painting, but the most curious fact concerns the mode of the Gorgon's presentation.

> Gorgo, the 'anti-face,' is represented only through a face... in an ineluctable confrontation of gazes... this antiprosopon is given over to the gaze in its fullness, with a clear demonstration of the signs of her dangerous visual effects (Frontisi-Ducroux, 1995, p. 68).
>
> (Agamben, 1999, p. 53)

Medusa's representations, and even the reflection of her face in Perseus' shield—as described in the myth—can be viewed as representing the imaginary; it is an "absolute image" (Agamben, 1999, p. 53). The myth itself, on the other hand, represents the symbolic, the myth's existence in language and culture through diverse traditions and to our present day. And, finally, the Gorgon's face, evoked in the representations and in the myth, but is not fully grasped by either, is the "Real" (Freud [1955] and Ferenczi [2002b] also referred to the Medusa head in relation to castration). This real dimension can only be evoked and never fully captured by language or image.

Regarding the notion of "confusion of tongues," and using the Lacanian concepts of imaginary, symbolic, and real (RSI), it is possible to extract from Ferenczi's writings three dimensions of the confusion of tongues: an imaginary dimension, established between the innocent child and the passionate adult, which subverts that state and is linked to the seduction fantasies present in psychic reality; a symbolic dimension, related to the confusion of tongues as a metaphor, as conceptualized by Rachman (1989); and a real dimension, which is the purely traumatic dimension. It can be seen how the traumatizing agent does not appear in the symbolic narration of the traumatic situation but in the real dimension that is hidden within the symbolic narration and the fantasies inherent in it.

Lacan believes that there is an incapacity of a "discourse"[11] to name something of the Real. There is a singular tongue in each human subject that is not part of the shared language, which is precisely lalangue. How can we access this tongue? Are there fixed senses in the unconscious, or can we liberate ourselves from that and read the unconscious in another way? For Lacan, writing is a resource for "unhearing" certain dimensions of a person's discourse, unhearing one's language and the sense inherent to it, in order to grasp the Real dimension of lalangue. Not only are there things to be heard, but there are elements of the unconscious to be read. Lacan develops the notion of "letter" (and, in this sense, the reference to writing) to think of elements in the unconscious that cannot be linked to other signifiers or representations. The question is: How can we access that Real, traumatic dimension of language that lies beyond the symbolic substrate of language?

In his seminar *Of a Discourse that would not be of the Semblant* (1971/2009), Lacan shows great interest in Chinese poetry, for it does not add elements but instead removes elements in order to produce an effect of indetermination. Because "the real is 'organized' or 'represented' through images and words that do not actually capture the real, but always misrepresent it" (Shepherdson, 2008, p. 28), he believes that emptying produces a greater "proximity" to the Real. He sees the creation of sculptures as being different from the creation of paintings, as sculpting consists of extracting elements. He believes that psychoanalysis should not add elements, i.e., meanings, but extract them in order to reach the dimension of the real that has not been captured or conquered by language.[12]

There are then two levels of trauma: the violent, intense, and unforeseeable experience, which cannot be symbolized;[13] and, before that (primordially or structurally), the symbolic order itself, which infests the infant's body and psyche through its erogenous zones. There is a "nameless dread" (Bion, 1962a, p. 309; 1962b, p. 96), as well as a "dread of the name."

Once, at the beginning of a seven-year analysis, and once near the end of treatment, my analysand had the following transference experience with language: he could hear that the analyst was saying something and that he was saying it at a volume at which he could hear it. He could identify that it was being said in a certain language he could understand, and he could even identify that the phrase was structured coherently and made sense, but he could not extract any meaning out of what was being said to him, even after the interpretation was repeated to him. He said he would not be able to repeat any of the words that had been said to him, even though he knew these words were familiar to him. There was a fracture, for the patient, in this experience, between the mechanics of language and the sense inherent to it. This experience made him anxious. He associated this event with a very early experience, before he controlled his sphincters, in which his father spoke to him; not only was he unable to extract any meaning from his words, but he felt his father's voice came to him in the form of oscillating jerks or waves (similar to a radio's volume being elevated and reduced intermittently), which was painful for his ears and was associated with intense anxiety.

Further in analysis, and accompanied by dreams, he spoke of a very deep and intense cry. Every time he linked this cry to sadness, I intervened to emphasize only "a cry," breaking the association of it to the adjective "sad." The analysand later stated that after a session, as he walked from my office, he was able to grasp the dimension of that cry with no sadness, or better, beyond sadness, feeling it intensely in his chest. He was able to grasp somatically that "primordial cry," as he called it, as the infant's most primitive reaction to need, before the response of an Other who could identify that cry as sadness. "It is like the Cheshire Cat's smile: a mouthless smile; an impossible," he said. A Real.

Ferenczi interprets his famous and frequently cited dream of the "wise" or "clever" baby (Ferenczi, 1923/2002a, p. 349) as a baby who knows of sexuality and can speak of it. But Ferenczi believes his interpretation is incomplete (Ferenczi, 1923/2002a, p. 349; see footnote), and this may authorize us to push it a little further. Isn't a newborn who speaks a baby who has managed to avoid the "trauma of language?" This baby is a subject who does not need to strive to find the signifiers who name him or her in the torrid terrains of the Other and whose body is not lacerated by the words and desire of that Other. The newborn would be the incarnation of a living "missing link" between the infans and the child.[14] In his *Child Language, Aphasia, and Phonological Universals*, Roman Jakobson (1968) termed the "apex of babble,"[15] (*die Blüte des Lallen*s) the capacity of the nonspeaking child to produce all of the possible sounds of the different tongues, a capacity that is lost as he or she emphasizes the sounds of the mother or native tongue, which, paradoxically, the child will acquire with great effort (Heller-Roazen, 2008, pp. 9–18).

In his *Clinical Diary*, Ferenczi describes what he intuits is the experience of the child before he or she becomes submerged in the scalding bath of language:

> The idea of the still half-dissolved state (consistency) of the childish personality tempts the imagination to suppose that the childish personality is in much closer contact with the universe, and therefore its sensitivity is much greater than that of the adult, crystallized into rigidity. It would not surprise us either if some day it were to be demonstrated that in this early state the whole personality is still resonating with the environment— and not only at particular points that had remained permeable, namely the sensory organs. So-called supernormal faculties—being receptive to processes beyond sensory perceptions (clairvoyance), apprehending the communications of an alien will (suggestion from a distance)—may well be ordinary processes, in the same way that animals (dogs), whose personalities evidently always remain in a state of dissolution, possess such apparently subnormal faculties (sense of smell at a colossal distance, the inexplicable adoption of the owners' sympathies and antipathies). Here the first possibility to understand the so-called telegony (the influence of the mother's psychic experiences on the child in the womb).
>
> (Dupont, 1988, p. 81)

Ferenczi was labelled a madman by Jones[16] (1953) and was marginalized by analysts of his time and by generations that followed until interest in his work finally returned, much like forgotten psychic material returns from the repressed. Isn't it a landscape of madness that precisely touches the boundaries of language? Lacan (1967) calls the madman the free man—he who has freed himself from the confines of the Other. For Ferenczi, insanity may be that which keeps us from dying (Orpha; Dupont, 1988, p. 8; Gutiérrez-Peláez, 2008a).

Effects on the Psychoanalytic Treatment

There are many examples of Lacan's clinical interventions in which he avoids the use of language. One example is given by Suzanne Hommel. In a recent film on Lacan, directed by Gerard Miller (2011), Hommel (a former analysand of Lacan) describes what it was like to be in analysis with him. Hommel tells us she was born in 1938 and therefore lived through the horrors of World War II, its anguish, the postwar period, the hunger, and the lies. She asked Lacan in one of her first sessions if she could ever get rid of the pain she felt, "Can I cure myself of this suffering?" for she had the idea that psychoanalysis could remove her pain. She says she knew by his silence to her question that this would not be possible, that she would have to deal with her suffering forever.

In analysis, she speaks of a dream: "Every day I wake up at 5 A.M." Then she adds: "At 5 A.M. the Gestapo came home looking for Jews." Immediately, Lacan stands up from his chair, walks to the couch where she lies and gently caresses her cheek. She understood how he had trans- formed the "Gestapo" into a "Geste-á-peau," a gesture on the skin, a gentle gesture. She experienced this as the transformation of that horrific representation— "Gestap"—into something kind and human, an extremely tender gesture.

This surprise did not reduce the pain, but trans- formed it into something else. The proof is that now, 40 years later, I still speak of this gesture. I still have it on my cheek. It is also a call to humanity.

(Miller, 2011)

The transformation produced by this "Geste-á-peau" carries with it the echoes of the trauma that has left an indelible mark. Lacan's gentle gesture is still on her cheek, as well as the scar left by the trauma.

Jacques-Alain Miller (2008) suggested, in a conference in Buenos Aires in 2008, that for Lacan, psychoanalysis was an experience and a logical deduction. For Freud, he points out, it was a cure; for Melanie Klein, it was interpreted as a communication; for Jung, it meant an elevation; and, for Anna Freud, a pedagogy and an orthopaedic (p. 276). Ferenczi is not mentioned in this list, but it could be hypothesized that for him, psychoanalysis was a healing, a healing of the primordial trauma, of the *Urtrauma*. This is an important divergence between Ferenczi and Lacan: for Lacan, psychoanalysis is not about healing. To Ferenczi, this healing meant recovering the unconfused tongues, making the infans speak, bringing the child back to life, to his or her elemental Thalassa. For Lacan, it is explicit: we are sick of language; Ferenczi (1932b) wrote, language is "an alien will" (p. 111).

Through analysis of his patients, Ferenczi intended to reach the hu- man order before language itself, an order linked with the universe, the inorganic, with an absence of splitting and an access to the "language of the organs" (Ferenczi, 1932b pp. 6–7), or the "anarchy of the organs" (pp. 69–70). In this sense, it can be understood why Ferenczi, as Lacan, needed to produce technical innovations, derived directly from clinical work: he wanted to gain access to a stratum of the patient's psyche through a "talking cure" that was—and is—beyond the grounds of language.

Notes

1 A first version of this article was published in: Gutiérrez-Peláez, M. (2015). Ferenczi's Anticipation of the Traumatic Dimension of Language: A Meeting with Lacan. *Contemporary Psychoanalysis*, *51*(1): 137–154. DOI: 10.1080/00107530.2015.957255
2 Finally, other fundamental concepts of Ferenczi's work, such as the "identification with the aggressor" (Frankel, 2002, 2004) and psychic splitting (Gutiérrez-Peláez, 2010), have also been extensively reviewed.
3 Excommunicated.
4 Barzilai (1997) and Granoff (2004) have explored other related aspects of Lacan's and Ferenczi's work.
5 Jouissance, translated in English as "enjoyment," must be understood differently from— and opposed to—what Freud conceptualized as the pleasure principle. Jouissance is beyond the pleasure principle. As stated by Zizek (1993), "enjoyment (*jouissance*,

Genuss) is not to be equated with pleasure (Lust): 'enjoyment is precisely 'Lust im Unlust'; it designates the paradoxical satisfaction procured by a painful encounter with a Thing that perturbs the equilibrium of the 'pleasure principle.' In other words, enjoyment is located 'beyond the pleasure principle'" (p. 280).

6 In Lacan, the big Other is the symbolic order itself, but, secondarily, it also designates "radical alterity, an other-ness which transcends the illusory otherness of the imaginary because it cannot be assimilated through identification" (Evans, 1996, p. 136).

7 If that rejection were successful, the infant would not enter into the symbolic order. It is not absolute either, for a substrate of lalangue prevails in the speaking subject.

8 Related to body temperature that changes with the variations in temperature of the environment.

9 "Bioanalysis" is a term used by Ferenczi. It can be found in Thalassa and in "Masculine and Feminine" (Ferenczi, 1930). It is also a term used by Freud in his obituary of Ferenczi. As Judit Mészáros (2014) states: "In his bioanalysis within his book Thalassa: A Theory of Genitality (Ferenczi, 1989/1924), he described the melding of the biological and psychological functioning of the human being. This work, which would become known simply as Thalassa, discusses the current emergence of the onto- and phylogenetic instinctive tendencies in the human sexual drive" (p. 6).

10 "Topology is increasingly seen as a radically non-metaphorical way of exploring the symbolic order and its interactions with the real and the imaginary. The Borromean knot, so called because the figure is found on the coat of arms of the Borromeo family, is a group of three rings which are linked in such a way that if any one of them is severed, all three become separated" (Evans, 1996, p. 19).

11 "Whenever Lacan uses the term 'discourse' (rather than, say, 'speech') it is in order to stress the transindividual nature of language, the fact that speech always implies another subject, an interlocutor. Thus the famous Lacanian formula, 'the unconscious is the discourse of the other' (which first appears in 1953, and later becomes 'the unconscious is the discourse of the Other') designates the unconscious as the effects on the subject of speech that is addressed to him from elsewhere; by another subject who has been forgotten, by another psychic locality (the other scene)" (Evans, 1996, p. 45).

12 Freud (1905/1953) referred to the analogy of painting and therapy, and psychoanalysis and sculpture: "There is, actually, the greatest possible antithesis between suggestive and analytic technique—the same antithesis which, in regard to the fine arts, the great Leonardo da Vinci summed up in the formulas: *per via di pone* and *per via di levare*. Painting, says Leonardo, works *per via di pone*, for it applies a substance—particles of colour—where there was nothing before, on the colourless canvas; sculpture, however, proceeds *per via di levare*, since it takes away from the block of stone all that hides the surface of the statue contained in it. In a similar way, the technique of suggestion aims at proceeding per via di pone; it is not concerned with the origin, strength and meaning of the morbid symptoms, but instead, it superimposes something—a suggestion—in the expectation that it will be strong enough to restrain the pathogenic idea from coming to expression. Analytic therapy, on the other hand, does not seek to add or to introduce anything new, but to take away something, to bring out something; and to this end concerns itself with the genesis of the morbid symptoms and the psychical context of the pathogenic idea which it seeks to remove" (pp. 260–261).

13 Ferenczi defines this as follows: "What is traumatic is the unforeseen, the unfathomable, the incalculable... Unexpected, eternal threat, the sense of which one cannot grasp, is unbearable" (Dupont, 1988, p. 171).

14 As Ferenczi wrote in his *Clinical Diary*: "In infants these protective devices are not yet developed, so that infants communicate with the environment over a much broader surface. If we had the means to get such a child to tell us what this hypersensitivity makes

him capable of, we would probably know much more about the world than our narrow horizon now allows" (Dupont, 1988, p. 148).

15 It is impossible not to link this "babble" of the child to that "Babel" of the "confusion of tongues" and the resonances of that Biblical myth in Ferenczi's paradigmatic paper (Gutiérrez-Peláez, 2012).

16 "After their meeting in the previous September, Freud and Ferenczi did not again discuss their differences. Freud's feeling for him never changed, and Ferenczi remained on at least outwardly friendly terms. They continued to exchange letters, the burden of which was mainly Ferenczi's increasingly serious state of health. The medical treatment was successful in holding the anemia itself at bay, but in March, the disease, as it sometimes does, attacked the spinal cord and brain, and for the last couple of months of his life he was unable to stand or walk; this undoubtedly exacerbated his latent psychotic trends" (Jones, 1953, p. 176; emphasis added).

Chapter 3

Sándor Ferenczi and Sándor Márai

The Hungarian Intelligentsia[1]

Introduction

If a single individual can embody a passion for clinical practice, for the limits and potentialities of the human psyche, for psychoanalysis, the unconscious, and madness, Sándor Ferenczi is the perfect circle. A distinguished disciple of Freud, he managed to stand out among his generation of psychoanalysts not only for his audacity. Ninety years after his death, his work has emerged from obscurity, and the extensive series of publications and academic events—both local and international—that continue to take place periodically forecast that his ideas will remain relevant for generations to come, contributing to the debates of the 21st century.

Family Background and Political Affiliations

Sándor Ferenczi's father, Bernath Fränkel, was Polish (born in Kraków) and arrived in Hungary as a teenager, seemingly fleeing the anti-Semitic pogroms spreading from Galicia (Johnson, 2004, p. 436). His mother, Rósa Eibenschütz, born in the same city as Bernath, grew up in Vienna after her family relocated there. Ferenczi's father was part of the patriotic forces that rose up in 1848 against the extension of Habsburg imperial power over Hungary during the failed Hungarian Revolution and the War of Independence of 1848–1849. This insurrection was quickly defeated, but Bernath remained in Hungary, settling in the city of Miskolcz. Michel Heilprin, an American immigrant, owned a bookstore in the city where Ferenczi's father worked, which he later purchased in 1956, transforming the bookstore into the family business. Thus, Sándor Fränkel was born on July 7, 1873, and grew up in the intellectual environment of this bookstore located in the city centre, which specialized in publishing and disseminating "radical and patriotic literature" (Stanton, 1997, p. 6). The bookstore became a major cultural hub, hosting diverse gatherings and concerts.

A few years before Sándor's birth, the Hungarians adopted Hungarian as their official language, as German had previously been the official language of the entire Habsburg Empire. Therefore, in 1879, Bernath changed his surname from Fränkel to Ferenczi, adopting the Hungarian linguistic convention.

DOI: 10.4324/9781003663324-3

Sándor was the eighth of 12 children. Sándor Ferenczi's biographers have often highlighted the early losses in his life (his younger sister, Vilma, died when he was eight years old, and his father passed away when he was 15) and how his mother, Rósa, devoted herself to the family bookstore with fervour, neglecting the care of a Sándor in need of maternal attention. At 21, Ferenczi graduated as a physician, already deeply interested in neurology and psychiatry. Drawing on the scientific texts of French medical literature, he developed an early interest in hypnosis and studies on hysteria. His first jobs were in the venereal disease unit of Rókus Hospital and the Elizabeth Hospice in Budapest.

In 1899, at the age of 26, he published the first of dozens of articles in the journal *Gyógyàszat* ("Therapy"), edited by Miksa Schächter, an important early influence on Ferenczi. This first article, titled "Spiritismus," set the tone for his early writings. His interests revolved around love, sexuality, hysteria, perversions, homosexuality, dreams, unconscious processes, the relationship between body and mind, and the evolution of the psyche (Erös, 2004, p. 126), among other topics.

Ferenczi lived for many years at the Royal Hotel (until his marriage to Gizella Palos on March 1, 1919, at the age of 46), located in central Budapest. The hotel's café was a gathering place for Hungary's intellectual elite, hosting prominent figures of the time, such as poet and writer Dezső Kosztolányi, writer and poet Sándor Márai (Mészáros, 2010, p. 69), journalist and writer Frigyes Karinthy, renowned painter of the "Group of Eight" Róbert Berény, psychoanalyst Lajos Levy, philanthropist and businessman Antal Freund Tószeghi (known as Anton von Freund), neurologist and psychoanalyst Imre Hermann, among others. Attendees of the Royal Hotel's "café gatherings" also included composer Béla Bartók, philosopher György Lukács, and anthropologist Géza Róheim (Jiménez Avello, 1998, p. 44).

Ferenczi engaged not only with the medical community but also with well-known artists, writers, and critics. Psychoanalysis, that "new science," operated as both a field and a discourse in which the significant questions and themes of this flourishing era were articulated and circulated. Other strong intellectual groups of the time included the Galileo Group, the Twentieth Century Group, and the Radical Intellectuals.

The level of discussion Ferenczi maintained with his interlocutors was remarkable, where ideas and viewpoints were not compromised for the sake of maintaining politeness. Some of these discussions transcended the intimate circle of the café and entered the public sphere. For instance, Karinthy, a famous journalist and writer of the time, apparently became disillusioned with certain aspects of psychoanalysis and advocated for other therapeutic methods that addressed the era's demands for efficacy and efficiency.

In 1924, Ferenczi (1924/1981) published a letter in the *Nyugat* ("West") newspaper (absent in the English edition of his works) addressing Karinthy, saying:

My dear Karinthy, [You] said that you knew of two types of scholars and two types of science. The first seeks truth and strives to awaken slumbering humanity; the other avoids disturbing the drowsy world's tranquility at all costs and even seeks to lull it into a deeper slumber. Psychoanalysis, you said, possesses a unique faculty for awakening people and seeks to give the human psyche, through knowledge, not only self-mastery but also mastery over organic and physical forces.

But now you write that analysis should cease in favor of studying those who speak of peace, harmony, and well-being, and that, with the help of skillful suggestions, even through a hypnotic dream, they surreptitiously introduce into the human psyche sensations, ideas, and reasonable, intelligent, comforting, and blissful intentions.

I initially found your words about the power of the wise man rather audacious, but since then, I have been convinced of their truth. I recognized the 'awakening' capacity inherent in psychoanalysis and have not changed my opinion, because I know that in the absence of authentic and courageous science, any effort to find happiness is futile and can only provoke a fleeting illusion. But you, on the other hand, seem to have lost patience (perhaps under the influence of current miseries), no longer desiring truth or science, and only aspire to provide our tormented world with a bit of happiness, at any cost, even if it means inducing slumber. In a word, I simply want to note here that, between the two of us, it is I who have not abandoned the ranks of those who awaken.

(p. 297–299)

This subjective position of Ferenczi as an "awakener" is undoubtedly one way to interpret his place in psychoanalysis. In his insistence on the analyst's training, on taking analysis to its conclusion, and on adapting the analytical framework and technique to the needs of the patient, Ferenczi unsettled the psychoanalytic establishment, which sought, in contrast, to establish fixed and immutable conventions for the proper course of psychoanalytic treatment.

History of the Hungarian Psychoanalytic Association and Its Interdisciplinary Nature

A century ago, on May 19, 1913, the Budapest Psychoanalytic Society was founded, with Ferenczi as president until his death, psychoanalyst István Hollós as vice president, and psychoanalyst Sándor Radó as secretary. Other members included Anton von Freund, psychoanalyst Lajos Levy (more interested in the psychoanalytic interpretation of biblical texts than in clinical practice and married to von Freund's sister) (Weibel, 2005, p. 529), and renowned poet Hugo Ignotus. This group clearly illustrates the significant interdisciplinarity of the Hungarian Psychoanalytic Society and how psychoanalysis was embedded at the heart of the intellectual ferment in early 20th-century Hungary. As Stanton (1997) points out, "From the outside, the Society appears quite subversive, containing outspoken and renowned advocates of global communism, homosexual rights, anti-militarism, and the imminent collapse of the Habsburg Empire" (p. 22).

Ignotus was the editor of the journal *Nyugat* ("The West"), a highly influential publication that was pivotal for Hungarian literature at the beginning of the century, with Desző Kosztolányi among its contributors and where his prolific career began. By 1918, when the Fifth Psychoanalytic Congress was held in Budapest—primarily addressing the topic of "war neuroses"—the Society had 20 members. Von Freund was a fundamental figure in organizing this Congress. A chemist by profession, von Freund was a wealthy industrialist, owner of the Kőbányai brewery, and contributed financial resources at various times, including for the establishment of a bookstore, a publishing house, and a clinic (Danto, 2005, pp. 21–24). Due to political upheavals following the Congress, the bookstore and publishing house were ultimately established in Vienna in 1920.

The scale and prominence of that Fifth Congress led Freud (2002/1918, p. 382) to write to Abraham, saying that he conceived Budapest as the great capital of psychoanalysis worldwide.

Although the war significantly limited attendance—with only 42 people in total—the Congress brought unprecedented recognition to the psychoanalytic movement:

> In contrast to the relative scarcity of participants, they were welcomed and celebrated with a grandeur never before seen by the relatively marginal psychoanalytic movement. For the first time in history, officials from three countries (Austria, Germany, and Hungary) attended the opening ceremony; participants were officially greeted by the city's mayor; the splendid hall of the Academy of Sciences was granted as the venue for their meetings; they were accommodated in the luxurious and then newly constructed Gellért Hotel and Spa; a boat (with an onboard orchestra) was made available to them for a river tour of Budapest; newspapers, cinematic newsreels, and medical journals all extensively covered the event. All this magnificence in how psychoanalysis was treated in Budapest, and the very fact that this city was chosen as the venue, was no coincidence but rather the logical reward for the merits achieved in Hungary and within the psychoanalytic community by Ferenczi.
>
> (Jiménez Avello, 1998, p. 139–40)

The intellectual group known as the Galileo Group, composed mainly of physicians and medical students, was familiar with Ferenczi, who had delivered lectures to them on multiple occasions. It was through the initiative of this group that medical students gathered a large number of signatures to petition for psychoanalysis to be taught in the Faculty of Medicine. The petition also included a request to create a Department of Psychoanalysis at the university, led by Sándor Ferenczi. In 1918, this request was submitted, but the university's Conservative Board rejected it.

The following year, with the establishment of the Hungarian Soviet Republic, led by Béla Kun, the Revolutionary Government Council approved the petition. The philosopher György Lukács, who was not particularly enthusiastic about psychoanalysis, signed the approval. Thus, Ferenczi became the first university professor of psychoanalysis, marking the first time in history that psychoanalysis had an institutional place in an educational establishment, with access to clinical practice in Budapest.

During the same period, Géza Róheim was appointed as "the first professor of Anthropology," and Revesz as "the first professor of Experimental Psychology" (Stanton, 1997, p. 29), all thanks to the university revolution led by Lukács. However, Hungary's political turmoil led to Ferenczi losing his position at the university within a few months, following the rise to power of Admiral Miklós Horthy and the issuance of a series of anti-Jewish measures, marking the onset of what became known as the "White Terror."

These measures also prompted many Hungarian psychoanalysts to leave the country in subsequent years, including Sándor Radó, Jenő Hárnik, Jenő Varga, Sándor Lóránd, and Melanie Klein (who had joined the Society in 1919). Later, several future Hungarian psychoanalysts also emigrated, including Róbert Bak, David Rapaport, Mihály Bálint, Alice Bálint, Franz Alexander, and Teréz Benedek, many of whom moved to Berlin and other destinations.

A Life Dedicated to Psychoanalysis

From his years of medical training, Ferenczi was deeply interested in Freud's work, whom he met personally on February 2, 1908 (Stanton, 1997, p. 12). He quickly became part of the psychoanalytic movement and, within it, advocated for the analysis of the psychoanalyst: "[The lack of analysis of the analyst] can lead to the intolerable situation where our patients are better analyzed than we are ourselves" (Ferenczi, 2012/1932e, p. 250; see also *Clinical Diary*, 1932c, p. 137).

He emphasized the need to carry out this analysis to its conclusion. Ferenczi posed crucial questions for psychoanalysis that remain highly relevant, such as the inquiry into the endpoint of analysis: "Analysis truly ends when there is no suspension by either the physician or the patient: analysis must die of exhaustion" (Ferenczi, 1984c/1928, p. 56).

Ferenczi pioneered the introduction of modifications to analytic technique, such as his renowned concepts of "relaxation and neo-catharsis" and his controversial "mutual analysis." He observed that not all patients adapted equally to the analytic framework. Known as an "expert in difficult cases" (Ferenczi, 1984b/1931), he understood psychosis and the need to approach it differently from traditional cases. His own passion for the unconscious, its potential for deciphering, and its limits drove him to introduce technical modifications as attempts to capture what manifested insistently in clinical experience and simultaneously eluded him.

The relationship between Freud and Ferenczi ended appallingly. Ferenczi had undergone analysis with Freud and reproached him for not accompanying him to the end of his analysis and for not allowing the negative transference to unfold. It was in the wake of Ferenczi's paper, *Confusion of Tongues Between Adults and the Child* (1984a/1932a and 2012/1932e), that the rupture between the two analysts became imminent. Freud accused Ferenczi of reverting to Freud's earlier trauma theory. This interpretation persisted among subsequent generations of analysts, some criticizing it, others exalting it.

However, Ferenczi was not merely returning to an earlier Freud; rather, he introduced innovative aspects—clinical, epistemic, and practical—that, over the years, have come to be recognized and appreciated. Ferenczi passed away from pernicious anaemia on May 22, 1933, at 2:30 P.M., shortly before his 60th birthday. He was buried two days later in the Farkasréti Jewish Cemetery in Budapest. His tombstone bears his name alongside a brief inscription in capital letters: "A PSZICHOANALIZIS MAGYAR MEGALAPITOJA," which translates to "THE FOUNDER OF PSYCHOANALYSIS IN HUNGARY."

The Legacy of Sándor Ferenczi

In the final volume of the *Standard Edition*, under the "Bibliography of Other Specialized Authors," Freud's references to Ferenczi's works are listed. "Ferenczi is mentioned sixty-nine times in Freud's work. These references are distributed across thirty-four of Freud's texts, and by coincidence, they also refer to thirty-four of Ferenczi's writings. These figures place him as the most frequently cited author" (Jiménez Avello, 1998, p. 28), and as the author whose works Freud engaged with the most.

Freud (1976b) wrote, on the occasion of Ferenczi's 50th birthday, that his analytical writings "are universally known and appreciated [...] Books and pamphlets written in Hungarian have had new editions and have familiarized analysis among Hungary's educated circles" (pp. 288–289).

Beloved by some and repudiated by others, Ferenczi remained faithful to his analytical rigour and, in a way, pushed the psychoanalytic movement as a whole to its limits, resembling a religious fanatic who becomes subversive to the very institution from which they originate. Freud (1976b) paid tribute to this analyst, patient, interlocutor, and colleague, stating: "Hungary, so geographically close to Austria yet so scientifically distant, has so far provided psychoanalysis with only one collaborator, S. Ferenczi; but such a one is worth an entire association" (p. 32). In the obituary Freud wrote in 1933, he referred to Ferenczi's writings as having "made disciples of all analysts" (Freud, 1976c, p. 227).

Kosztolányi, reflecting on Ferenczi after his death (quoted by Mészáros, 2000), remarked:

> He suffered from an intense restlessness, a childlike playfulness, and an insatiable curiosity [...] He was deeply interested in linguistics, theatre, new ideas, gossip—any human matter [...] No one could suggest something seemingly

improbable without him finding it plausible, nor could anyone present a truth so well-founded that he couldn't insert a halo of doubt [...] He even regarded humanity itself as a puzzle that could not be described using one or another psychological paradigm.

(p. 54)

Ernest Jones' biography of Freud (1953) left a damaging legacy by portraying Ferenczi in his later years as psychotic, an attempt to discredit his work. After Ferenczi's death, his 1931-2 paper *Confusion of Tongues Between Adults and the Child* was actively suppressed by several psychoanalysts of the time, excluding it from public knowledge (Gutiérrez-Peláez, 2012; Hidas, 1993; Masson, 1984; Rachman, 1989; Sylwan, 1984).

Regarding the history of Ferenczi's works in other languages, "the last 'English edition' of his work was produced in the 1950s, based largely on translations made around 1920. Unfortunately, many of these now appear poorly dated and inaccurate. The edition is also incomplete, as many early Hungarian articles, some German lectures, and most reviews remain untranslated. Finally, the work is not chronologically ordered, lacks cross-references, and is insufficiently edited to clarify forgotten details of old debates" (Stanton, 1997, p. 57).

The *Clinical Diary* (1985/1932c and 1997/1932d), perhaps the most unusual and singular psychoanalytic text in history, first appeared in French in 1985, translated by Judith Dupont. That same year, it was published in Spanish, translated by Beatriz Castillo in an edition by Editorial Conjetural, and later in 1997, with a translation by José Luis Etcheverri, in an edition by Amorrortu titled *Sin simpatía no hay curación* (*Without Sympathy, There is No Healing*) (1932d), a title derived from a note in the *Diary*. It was not until 1988 that the *Clinical Diary* was published for the first time in German, the language in which it was originally written.

That year also saw the first English edition, translated by Michael Balint and published by Harvard Press, which restored sections Balint had omitted in the original. Thanks to Judith Dupont's efforts, other editions now include this material.

In Spanish, the Horné publishing house in Argentina released *Sexo y psicoanálisis* (*Sex and Psychoanalysis*) in 1959, and Paidós published *Teoría y técnica del psicoanálisis* (*Theory and Technique of Psychoanalysis*) in 1967 (Sabsay Foks, 2011, p. 429). Ferenczi's *Collected Works* were translated by Francisco Javier Aguirre and published by Espasa-Calpe. The first three volumes of this edition appeared in 1981, and the fourth in 1984. However, the *Clinical Diary* was not included in this fourth volume. In 2012 (Gutiérrez-Peláez, pp. 263–276), a new translation of the article *Sprachverwirrung zwischen den Erwachsenen und dem Kind* (1933a/1932b) [*Confusion of Tongues Between Adults and the Child*] corrected errors in earlier Spanish translations, which had been based on English or French versions.

It is safe to assume that Ferenczi will continue to provoke discussion for future generations and will remain a figure of both love and controversy. As his work continues to be revisited and published, contemporary readings of both classic and lesser-known texts will shed new light on psychoanalytic theory. For example,

Judith Mészáros published in 1999, for the first time, an edition of Ferenczi's pre-psychoanalytic writings (Erös, 2004, p. 128), which have been the subject of limited study and, in 2022, the complete preanalytic writings from 1897 to 1908 (Mészáros, Harmatta & Bókay, 2022). In 2012, during the *International Ferenczi Conference: The Faces of Trauma* in Budapest, Emanuel Berman (University of Haifa, Israel) and Martha Fülöp (Institute of Cognitive Neuroscience and Psychology of the Hungarian Academy of Sciences) presented a paper titled *The Unknown Poet: Sándor Ferenczi*, inspired by a series of poems recently discovered by Blaise Plasztory, the grandson of Gizella Ferenczi's brother. Written in a single notebook, some adorned with his drawings, these writings were never intended for publication yet were preserved. The researchers' conclusion: "Ferenczi was a very poor poet!" underscores that his rediscovery as a writer is unlikely, and his poetry from those years seems to hold little promise. However, these works, along with his drawings, could fit within the *Outsider Art* genre. They undoubtedly reveal particular aspects of their author—an intense, visceral, jealous lover—and the researchers plan to publish some of these poems in the future, accompanied by a study on Ferenczi's life during this period. Nonetheless, as stated by Fergusson & Gutiérrez-Peláez (2022, p. 104):

it would be unfair to disregard Ferenczi's 'poetry' through this marginal examples. A poet is, amongst other things, someone who can transform words from its common use and articulate and blend them in a novel way that can lead to understanding and grasping the sense of reality and existence that is elusive to thought and comprehension. His probing into the traumatic dimension of language is what certainly inserts him into his poetic talent and were we can more clearly find the poetic aspect of the psychoanalytic act. His *Diary* was, as he mentioned in his correspondence with Freud, his "scientific 'poetry and truth'.

Obituary by Sándor Márai

Given Ferenczi's central role in the Hungarian intellectual scene, several of the greatest thinkers of his time wrote about his untimely death. Among them was the renowned Hungarian writer Sándor Márai, who published a brief obituary titled "The Living and the Dead." However, referring to it simply as an obituary would be misleading, as Márai's text is astonishingly vibrant. In it, he reflects on various aspects of Sándor Ferenczi, with the following points standing out:

The Personality of Ferenczi

Márai writes:

[Ferenczi] instructed one of his family members that, should he die suddenly, they should not believe it immediately and should shake him vigorously... This is what he thought about the body; as if it were a clock that stops now and then and needs a shake to start again. In this cold arrogance, reflected in the instructions he gave his family regarding his own death, the entirety of the man is revealed.

He continues: "He knew what poets know: how to touch that inexpressible something that constitutes the true secret of a soul, of a life."

The Subversive and Marginal Nature of Psychoanalysis

Márai's lucidity on this subject is remarkable and remains highly relevant historically:

Why, then, does everyone hate this new science with such infinite intensity: the Bolsheviks consider it 'counter-revolutionary'; Hitler and his followers find it harmful and revolutionary; the American bourgeois critics see it as 'Jewish science'; and the Church placed it on the Index for 'breaking' the unity of the spirit, for 'eroding' faith?

This observation highlights how psychoanalysis, from its very inception, was perceived as subversive to institutions and political systems. It also underscores how, when psychoanalysis becomes too comfortable within an institution, it is likely that something other than psychoanalysis is being practised in its name. Freud himself had forewarned about this in a letter to Reik regarding his journey to the United States, advising him to be cautious of those colleagues for whom "psychoanalysis is nothing more than a servant of psychiatry" (1938, cited by Gay, 1989, p. 701).

Ferenczi's Fundamental Role in the Intellectual Landscape of His Time

Márai is unequivocal in his assessment:

Ferenczi belongs in the gallery of Hungarian intellectual figures of the century, just as much as his teacher and friend Freud belongs to the history of the 20th century [...] The importance of the discovery [of the unconscious] is on par with that of gunpowder, the printing press, or the theory of relativity. This is what Ferenczi brought to light [...] Without Freud, and without what Ferenczi refined and added, it would be impossible to imagine the intellectual radiography of this century.

These short excerpts provide a glimpse into the profound impact Ferenczi had on the Hungarian intellectual landscape and how he was perceived by his contemporaries. This contrasts starkly with the subsequent years, when his work fell into complete obscurity, only to return to the debates of psychoanalysis in the manner of repressed material resurfacing.

Márai's Own Repression and Rediscovery

Like Ferenczi, Márai's work also faced neglect and suppression in his homeland. When Ferenczi died, Márai was a young writer in his 30s, already enjoying considerable prestige. As his biographer Ernö Zeltner (2001) recounts, at that time:

> This novelist already had a substantial readership, which continued to grow thanks to his journalistic activities. Márai's name increasingly appeared in public life: he had achieved a prominent position and led an active life.
>
> (p. 97)

A staunch critic of totalitarian regimes and an opponent of the German occupation of Hungary, Márai eventually spent his final years in exile in the United States, in San Diego, California. His work was censored in Hungary. On February 21, 1989, Márai took his own life, unable to witness the events later that year that would surely have delighted him: the fall of the Berlin Wall. Six days before shooting himself, he wrote a heart-wrenching entry in his journal, the only handwritten note: "I am waiting for the call to arms; I am not in a hurry, but I don't want to postpone anything because of my doubts. The time has come" (Márai, 2008, p. 209).

The obituary written following Ferenczi's death was first published in the newspaper *Brassói Lapok* ("The Brassó Papers"), named after Márai's hometown, on June 14, 1933. It was reprinted in 1999 in the journal *Thalassa* and in 2000 in Judit Mészáros's book *In Memoriam Sándor Ferenczi*. The author, director of the Sándor Ferenczi Society in Budapest, authorized the translation and publication of this text into Spanish, marking the first time it has been translated into a language other than Hungarian. Here we present an English translation of Sándor Márai's (1999) "The Living and the Dead," a true gem that situates Ferenczi in the foundational place he occupies in the history of psychoanalysis.

The Living and the Dead[2]
        Sándor Márai

I already hate checking the morning news; I fear answering the phone: these days, not a week goes by without someone I care about passing away. After a certain age—even if the calendar still counts this age as youth—the attraction one feels for others is astonishingly restricted; everything and everyone goes through a sieve. One day, you wake up and realize that you are partly irrevocably alone, and partly part of an irrevocable, strange family, more genuine than the blood family: it is only a few people, both living and dead, whom you have encountered in the pagan chaos of the world, and one day you find out that, inevitably, they are connected to you.

In this other family, too, there is a parental hierarchy, there is a father and mother, respect and authority, jealousy and controversy; and the essence of this small, non-blood-related family is that you belong to it without a shadow of a doubt. It is not important to see them often; this other, more genuine family lacks the intimacy of cohabitation. Years may pass without the members of this family seeing each other, and when they do, they only exchange the obligatory words. For me—and for many others—Sándor Ferenczi belonged to this other family, because he was an exceptional teacher.

He passed away the week after Krúdy's death on a Monday night, still not sixty years old. My family shrinks... I mean, every week someone leaves me. (There is something sinister about this May; the weather is cold, shivering, unsettling. I write this because man does not live solely rationally.) The thirty-year-olds declaim grandly and legitimately, but it seems to me that the sixty-year-olds do not endure life with special resilience either. Ferenczi's death affected me in a completely primitive way: I did not believe it. When I hung up the phone after receiving the news, after brief meditation, I called my informant again to ask if they might have been mistaken. Later, I thought about it and realized that Ferenczi's death wounds and angers me; the childish idea animated me that he had invented something that did not apply to him; he could only die when he wanted to. I understood that he still didn't want to. (Through an alternate path, I learned how little he wanted to die and how much he despised death and the primitive structure of life: he instructed one of his family members that, in case he happened to die, they shouldn't immediately believe it and should shake him vigorously... That was what he thought of the body; as if it were a clock that stops occasionally and needs to be shaken to keep running. In this cold arrogance, where he gave his family instructions in case of his own death, the man in his entirety is completely reflected.)

That was also the reason his death wounded me. Perhaps it was simply that they had not shaken him as they should have.

Ferenczi belongs to the gallery of figures of Hungarian intellectuals of the century, at least as much as his teacher and friend Freud belongs to the history of the twentieth century. Whether analysis is therapy or not is hard to determine today; at this moment, I think it is more art than therapy. When Tolstoy wrote *War and Peace*, it was likely that later in his life he would not write nonsense, but there was no guarantee that his next novel would also be a masterpiece; as it wasn't, and only with *The Death of Ivan Ilyich* did he manage to create something that came close. In some way, this is how I see the practical possibilities of analysis: some well-conducted analyses are true, genius masterpieces. Freud or Ferenczi might perform a miracle two or three times in their lives, but the miracle requires the harmonious concurrence of experience, luck, the patient's quality, and many other unpredictable factors, which make it hard today to speak of routine therapy. In my opinion, the importance of analysis does not lie in its therapeutic certainty.

What Freud discovered, when he, along with Charcot, realized that the hysterical patient reproduces hysteria symptoms even in unconscious states, is where those symptoms retreat when the patient is disconnected from their consciousness and will. He asked the question and provided the answer: to the unconscious. Ferenczi discovered this in parallel and had the courage to accept the consequences of the discovery. Great intellectual acts are not just about genius and competence; they are the consequence of moral bravery. Without Freud and without what Ferenczi refined and added, it would be impossible to imagine the intellectual radiography of this century.

The little word 'inhibition' is already used by conservative politicians who burn psychoanalytic literature in the marketplaces and do not know that this word, as Freud pronounced it in his time, illuminated the new intellectual constellation of the world.

In Hungary, it was Sándor Ferenczi who carried out the work of cleansing that was vehemently rejected by official science everywhere. What does it mean to be an analyzed person? We can give a short answer: to be an individual without illusions. Is the analyzed person asocial? According to Freud and Ferenczi, no; they are even more social than the guild-type person who seeks shelter and refuge in the herd.

Why, then, does everyone hate this new science with the same infinite intensity: Bolsheviks consider it "anti-revolutionary"; Hitler and his people, harmful and revolutionary; American bourgeois critics see it as "Jewish science"; the Church placed it on the Index because it "breaks" the unity of the spirit, "erodes" faith? The loneliness of Freud and Ferenczi was ghostly, and the isolation of psychoanalysis is still indisputable today. Nevertheless, *The Interpretation of Dreams* is thirty years old and stands firm, like a rock, no matter how much they try to topple it; today it already has lexical importance. Analysis is not a solution because there is no solution. Analysis simply established something positive that we did not know before; it incorporated an X in the investigation of the soul, without which one cannot advance: the concept of the unconscious. This was Freud's contribution. The importance of the discovery has the same value as gunpowder, the printing press, or the theory of relativity. This is what Ferenczi highlighted.

At sixty years old, he dedicated forty to teaching and healing. Of course, without a chair, without a title, initially ridiculed, later hated. In our country, they do not even suspect the importance of his work. He was the one who most decisively fought the charlatans of psychoanalysis: he formed a kind of small, orthodox circle of selected doctors that did not admit people who wanted to make a business of analysis, as if it were an eccentric fashion. No doctor attended his burial; only his analyst friends accompanied him. He knew more about human life than any previous soul researcher in Hungary. I suspect he was a poet. Not that he wrote verses. But he knew what poets know: how to touch that inexpressible something that constitutes the true secret of a soul, of a life. When I was with him, I was always waiting to see if he would express it. He never did; he died first. I feel that I was left without an answer. That is why his death outrages me.

Notes

1 A first version of this chapter was published in: Gutiérrez-Peláez, M. (2013). Sándor Ferenczi y la intelectualidad húngara del siglo XX. *Affectio Societatis, 10*(18), 247–267.
2 The following is Marai's obituary, translated into English from the Spanish version of the original Hungarian text.

Chapter 4

Sándor Ferenczi and Jacques Derrida

On Confusion of Tongues[1]

On Babel and the Tower of Babel

What is known about the Tower of Babel? According to the Bible (Genesis 10:1–32 and 11:1–9), Noah begat Shem, who begat Cush, who in turn begat Nimrod, the first mighty one on Earth. Nimrod spearheaded the construction of the Tower of Babel, a tower of immense proportions that reached into the heavens. Some images of how this has stuck humanity's imagination are preserved in remarkable works of art: two of the three paintings by Brueghel "The Elder," the image by Monsu Desiderio, Frans Francken the Younger, and the 12th-century tablet from Salerno Cathedral, to name a few.

> It can be said that even though numerous representations of it are preserved and scattered across Europe from the High Middle Ages (in the capitals of the Doge's Palace and Monreale Cathedral, in the stained glass of Saint Martin of Colmar, in the murals of Saint-Savin-sur-Gartempe, in the Campo Santo of Pisa by Benozzo Gozzoli), its image has a certain localization in time and space: in Germany, the Netherlands, and Flanders at a time when their peoples were separating from Rome.
>
> (Benet, 1990, p. 17)

Other examples include: the anonymous panel from the Prague Museum, the Berning panel in the Mauritshuis in The Hague; those by Bril and Kaulbach in the Dahlem Museum of Berlin; those by Van Cleef, also in Prague; Van Troyen in the Gemäldegalerie of Dresden; and Jan van Scorel. It seems that although representations of the Tower of Babel are unknown until the Cotton Bible of the fifth or sixth century, it is from Brueghel "The Elder" onward that the tower becomes a central subject in painting. Between 1550 and 1650, numerous altarpieces referencing the tower appear.

However, these creations are not of interest to us as works of art, nor for their aesthetic value, but because they themselves constitute translations. But is it possible, from this multiplicity of representations, to reconstruct the entirety of the tower? Is the sum of translations—whether pictorial, lyrical, or semantic—sufficient to reconstruct the *Urbild* of Babel?

DOI: 10.4324/9781003663324-4

According to the American writer Paul Auster (1985):

As for the Tower itself, legend had it that one third of the structure sank into the ground, one third was destroyed by fire, and one third was left standing. God attacked it in two ways in order to convince man that the destruction was a divine punishment and not the result of chance. Still, the part left standing was so high that a palm tree seen from the top of it appeared no larger than a grasshopper. It was also said that a person could walk for three days in the shadow of the Tower without ever leaving it. Finally [...] whoever looked upon the ruins of the Tower was believed to forget everything he knew.

(p. 45)

Milton (1667, p. 108) reveals another image:

But God, who oft descends to visit men
Unseen, and through their habitations walks
To mark their doings, them beholding soon,
Comes down to see their city, ere the tower
Obstruct Heaven-towers, and in derision sets
Upon their tongues a various spirit, to rase
Quite out their native language; and, instead,
To sow a jangling noise of words unknown:
Forthwith a hideous gabble rises loud,
Among the builders; each to other calls
Not understood; till hoarse, and all in rage,
As mocked they storm: great laughter was in Heaven,
And looking down, to see the hubbub strange,
And hear the din: Thus was the building left
Ridiculous, and the work Confusion named.

What was the purpose of such an impressive feat? To forge their own name, a name for humanity. Babel, Derrida explains (1985), is confusion, but it is also the City of God (Ba: Father; Bel: God) (p. 36). Consequently, humans fail to forge their own name, as God descends and gives them his own (imposing and opposing it), namely, Confusion, thereby bringing about the confusion of tongues.

Thus, God's name as the name of the Father, by giving his name and subsequently all names, gives rise to language, but "one can no longer understand oneself when there is only a proper name, and one can no longer understand oneself when there is no longer a proper name" (Derrida, 1985, p. 36), leading to the reign of confusion of tongues in the city of Babel. The unpronounceable name YHWH leads to the dispersion and multiplication of tongues. It is this singular name of God as the name of the Father that imposes the mark of Inalienability on language, namely, its confusion.

As Benjamin suggests, translation is law and imposes an unpayable debt that must be paid, "becoming something necessary and impossible as a result of a struggle for the appropriation of the name, something necessary and forbidden in the interval between two absolutely proper names" (Derrida, 1985, p. 39). The name of God is confused in language in such a way that it comes to signify confusion.

Moving from one language to another appears as a feat that tends toward the absurd. But it does not always occur from one language to another; sometimes many languages speak within one language, and the polyphony of phrases overflows the possibilities offered by the literalness of languages and their word-for-word correspondence. Thus, a particular semantic order registers polyvalence in its multilingual resonance (as in Joyce's *Finnegans Wake* example brought up by Derrida, where *he war* means "war" in English and "was" in German, or in the title of the work itself, where reading *Finnegans* with or without an apostrophe—either as possessive or as Finn-again, Finn-anew—alters its meaning, and *Wake* can signify a funeral or an awakening) (Boorstin, 1994, p. 648).

The Akkadian significance of Babel seems to have been "Gate of God." This etymological account of the word is traced by Parrot (1961) in *The Tower of Babel*, a study ranging from cuneiform texts about ziggurats to the writings of Herodotus of Halicarnassus. He also conducts his own translation exercise, arguing that the word "babel" in Hebrew tradition comes from *balal*, meaning both "confuse" and "mix." He further suggests that "it seems to be a direct and certain copy from the Akkadian *bab-ilu* (Gate of God)" (p. 14). This latter meaning, no less significant, has also taken root and gained transcendence in the imagination of languages.

For this reason, it is interesting that the same word is read today in the multiplicity of languages, revealing a particular dimension of proper names, as if they belonged to a sphere distinct from regular language. It crosses and simultaneously deceives meanings, as Babel at least enjoys its double nature: being both a proper name and a common name, the name of God the Father and confusion. And it is even more confusing as *confusion* because, through its semantic correspondence (a kind of intra-linguistic translation), it also becomes a proper name, namely, Confusion as the name of God the Father. Hence, "a proper name, in its proper sense, does not properly belong to the language" (1985, p. 40) and only does so by allowing itself to be translated into its semantic meaning within the language. Consequently, the proper name is inscribed as no longer proper.

According to Benet (1990), in his text *The Construction of the Tower of Babel*, three myths of autonomous and distinct natures converge around the tower: the existence of a single race with a single language, the purpose of constructing a tower that would reach the heights of heaven, and the divine decision to abort the project, destroy the utopia, and enact a second expulsion from paradise (p. 50). Thus, the dimension of translation appears as the same text being subject to the production of diverse meanings. It is also the dimension of the text as inexhaustible, that is, as capable of being translated as many times as what is introduced into it insists on (and demands) translation.

Translation and Hypnosis: Psychoanalytic Articulators in Babelian Confusion

Babel, which is Confusion, produces the confusion of tongues. "And the proper name of God [namely, YHWH] is already divided in the language sufficiently to also mean, confusedly, *'confusion'*" (Derrida, 1985, p. 39). In the history of psychoanalysis, there is already a precedent for this phrase, namely, Ferenczi's article (1932a) *Confusion of Tongues Between Adults and the Child.* It is remarkable that critics or commentators of Ferenczi have only rarely highlighted the Babelian resonances suggested both in the title and in the body of the article.

In his article, Ferenczi describes a dimension of confusion: the tender language of the child is confused with the language of the adult's passion. There is a confusion of tongues in the sense that the child's tender impulses are read as passionate by the adult, who reacts based on their own sexual dispositions, which are entirely different from those accessible and possible for the child due to their condition as an infant. The child, gripped by fear, submits and identifies with the aggressor. This causes a clear rupture in the child's psyche, who becomes both aggressor and victim, feeling an irreconcilable guilt and pain. A psychic fragmentation has occurred in the child to preserve the functioning of their psyche; such is the paradox presented by the author.

Moreover, in that article, another dimension of this confusion of tongues is highlighted, and this time it is Balint, Ferenczi's disciple and translator of his works into English, who incurs it: he conflates *Sprache* (language) and *Zunge* (tongue) into a single signifier, *tongue.* Balint seems unable to escape the ancient English translation of the Bible, which also incorporates this conflation, whereas Ferenczi avoids it in his article by employing both *Zunge* and *Sprache.* Spanish, however, is free of this confusion, which English does not exempt: in Spanish, *lengua* refers both to the organ of speech (anatomical) and to language. In other languages, such as Hebrew, it is not the tongue that speaks but the lip.

Translation has always been a central axis of psychoanalytic thought. Freud (1938) suggested:

> *We see that everything newly deduced by us must in turn be translated into the language of our perceptions, from which we can never free ourselves. When we say: 'Here an unconscious memory has intervened,' what we mean is: 'Here something completely incomprehensible to us has occurred, but if it had reached consciousness, we could only have described it thus and thus.'*
>
> (p. 198)

In the myth of Babel, the transformation of materials is also a form of translation: brick into stone and asphalt into mortar (Derrida, 1987, p. 37). The psychoanalyst faces, in practice and thought, the problems of translation: ensuring that the patient's language is not confused with their own. They also confront the problem raised by Derrida regarding how to translate a text written in multiple languages.

What the patient brings to sessions as discourse, trying to account for their own words, is often a great polyphony of voices speaking through their mouth.

Hypnosis is undoubtedly a central theme in psychoanalysis, far from being excluded from its sphere simply because Freud discarded it as a therapeutic method. If anything, the everyday clinical experience shows that hypnosis is the predominant factor, though in a manner quite different from that of Breuer, Janet, and early Freud. Perhaps it was also Ferenczi (1932b), who, when speaking of the "right path to liberation: demecanization and dehypnotization" (p. 100), most clearly summarized the continued relevance of hypnosis. Patients arrive at sessions already hypnotized, acting as though the words of others are their own, dictating their destinies like commands.

The principal characteristic of hypnosis involves the effect of words on a person who acts on another's orders as if they were their own, leaving no trace of the one who, like a puppeteer of words, manipulates the will that the hypnotized has relinquished. The function of hypnosis is transformed: how does one impose it on patients who already harbour it within themselves?

Thus, the polyphony of others' voices that the patient brings, unaware of the alien nature of these words in their hypnotic trance, compels the psychoanalyst to undertake a slow and cautious labour of dissection and reconstruction, guiding the patient's awakening and returning the words to those who first pronounced them, which the patient had incorporated as law. In this sense, the much-criticized *Küsstechnik* or "kiss technique" by Ferenczi could be re-read: the kiss as a metaphor for that place where tongues—or lips, if we adhere to the literalness of the Hebrew translation—converge, which in this context would be understood as the accurate officiation of translation:

> Let us follow this movement of love, the gesture of this lover (*liebend*) who operates in translation. It does not reproduce, restitute, or represent; essentially, it does not return the meaning of the original except at that point of contact or caress, the infinitely small of meaning. It extends the body of languages, expands tongues in symbolic extension; and symbolic here means that, however little restitution is carried out, the greater, the new whole must still reconstruct something.
>
> (Derrida, 1985, p. 55)

Thus, when Freud was alarmed by the words of Ferenczi's patient, who declared in social circles, "I have permission to kiss Papa Ferenczi as often as I wish" (*Clinical Diary*, cited by Stanton, 1997, p. 49), one might argue that Freud (in his own translation) did not read between the lines, or at least not beyond the specifics of transference love. These words could be re-read, and here we enter complex terrain, for it is unclear whether one translates or interprets, or whether these two even belong to different registers.

At the very least, one can state a certain correspondence between them, and it may be less risky to affirm that if an interpretation is correct, it is because something has converged at the level of languages. But whether it was an act of interpretation or a transgression of the patient's words, one might read, in this context, that her analysis included a level of understanding through lips precisely because, through Ferenczi's voice, she could hear the echo of her own desire and not its denial through his words, which would lead only to repeating the situation that had established the trauma. If we adhere to the literalness of the Hebrew translation, where tongue is referred to as *lip*, and understand the kiss as a dimension of love, of its operation, it can be seen that in the opening of the lip disposed to a kiss, the dimension of the gap is revealed, the breach that remains exempt and untouched in translation, which is paradoxically the very motor of translation.

Ferenczi understood this clearly. He stated, "Speech is telling the story of the trauma" (1932b, p. 163), articulating trauma as a trauma of language. Ferenczi recognized the role and value of love in the union of parts, knowing that "without sympathy, there is no healing" (1932b, p. 277). As an expert analyst in difficult cases, he confronted the shapelessness of the fragmented mind daily in his practice, appearing as a "shattered amphora," to use Benjamin's metaphor cited by Derrida (1985):

> Just as the fragments of an amphora, to reconstruct the whole, must be contiguous in the smallest details yet not identical to one another, so translation, rather than resembling the sense of the original, must, moved by love, and down to the detail, incorporate into its own language the original's mode of seeing things: in this way, as the fragments become recognizable as parts of the same amphora, the original and translation become recognizable as fragments of a greater language.
>
> (p. 55)

This greater language, in the case of psychoanalysis, would relate to one's own desire, to grasping something of the correspondence that exists between one's own words and the authenticity of the desire expressed through them. This is where the love of the analyst and that of the translator come into play, who, in this context, are merged into the same entity, uniting the parts, the voices, and the enunciation of the voices that populate discourse, bringing them into the modes of being of one's own language. The dimension of love in analysis has been resignified beyond transference love, which could only understand the *Küsstechnik* as an encounter of erogenous zones (skin, pores, and flesh) and not of tongues (without organs, to use a concept Gilles Deleuze borrowed from Antonin Artaud). "Let us not forget that Babel names a struggle for the survival of the name, of the language, or of the lips" (Derrida, 1985, p. 50). There exists an autonomy of the translated work from the original work. As stated at the beginning, the subject of translation acquires a debt (unpayable) to the work that demands the production of the translation. But the translated text is not an inscription of the same writing in another language or a transformation into the codes of another language. It is, above all, another text. Precisely, "the bond or obligation of debt does not occur between a donor and a donee but between two texts (two 'productions' or two 'creations'), creating a 'rigorous duality between the original and the version'" (Derrida, 1985, p. 47). Translations take on a life of their own and emerge as autonomous texts.

Granoff (1988) asserts that "Strachey produced nothing less than a work that *de facto* competes with Freud's. His work stands out above Freud's in the mental and psychic market of reading and teaching" (p. 167). Willson (2004) states that: "According to Foucault, Hyppolite's translation was so imbued with Hegel that even the Germans themselves turned to it to understand what, 'for a moment at least, became the German version'" (p. 16). Thus, translation, far from being an image or copy, does not appear as the representation or reproduction of the other from which it originates.

Much can be re-read, rewritten, and produced in psychoanalysis when hypnosis and translation are taken as lenses for interpretation. When Benjamin says that the text does not produce its recipients and translators but rather demands and summons them to the place of imposing the law—the law of translation (always failed)—a dimension is opened for thinking about the analytical demand. In this sense, the analysand appears as that which is to be translated, not by the analyst as representation, but by the position they occupy in relation to the analytic apparatus. What is fundamental in this demand for translation does not traverse the path of what is said, enunciated, communicated, or even the subject matter. Derrida's reading of Benjamin offers a perspective on translation, starting with the sacred text, where communication is not essential: "What does a literary work (*Dichtung*) 'say'? What does it communicate? Very little to those who understand it" (cited by Derrida, 1985, p. 48). Thus, when Winnicott (1954), irritated by the misinterpretable assertion that "the analyst is an artist," asks, "What patient would want to be someone else's poem or painting?" (p. 394), it should be clarified that this is not in terms of the analyst's creation, i.e., as a production based on the words they enunciate. Such an approach would lead back to hypnosis. Instead, it is about being understood within the equivalence of languages, in the displaced convergence of one language with another—the patient's and the analyst's—where something of the patient's own voice can be recovered.

The demand for translation exists (and is required) even before the translator appears; it is, one might say, inherent in the structure of the original. The debt does not obligate one to present a copy or a faithful representation of the original. The analyst is not obligated to either represent or communicate, and yet there is the analytic pact that binds and obligates both parties. If, as Lacan proposes, the unconscious is structured like a language, then it necessarily calls for a translation of what it says. Perhaps the very nature of the unconscious, as that which incessantly pushes forth, contains within itself elements akin to what Benjamin designates as "that which is to be translated."

The original does not appear fixed in time but is also subject to the laws of mutation, becoming, and multiple transformations.

The original is given by modifying itself; this gift is not of a given object—it lives and survives in mutation: 'For in its survival, which would not deserve this name if it were not mutation and renewal of the living, the original modifies itself. Even in the case of highly crystallized words, there is still a post-maturation.'

(Derrida, 1985, p. 50)

It is not possible to delve into all the pathways that Derrida's text illuminates for thinking about psychoanalysis. Clearly, this is not its aim, at least not in this writing. For now, we must settle for a mere mention. The idea of the mutation of the original, its modification, suggests for psychoanalysis the multiplicity of possible analytic interventions. It also leads us to think about the nature of the end of analysis as never fully concluded, always permitting the post-maturation of what seemed firmly established. This raises the question of how we can conceptualize the termination of an analysis. Even though there will always be words, and the text never truly falls silent, we nonetheless encounter what Ferenczi referred to, in the context of analysis, as its "exhaustion."

The end of analysis, thinking of analysis as translation, would not occur through the analysand's identification with the analyst, since translation does not reproduce but rather increases in its capacity to speak for itself, different from what would be a child subjecting themselves to the law of reproduction. Reproduction, precisely, would lie on the side of hypnosis; the capacity to speak for oneself, as different, on the other hand, lies on the side of dehypnotization. Benjamin is interested in the kinship between languages, but not as a historian might approach it. Instead, he explores that enigmatic relationship between one language and another. "Translation would not aim to say this or that, to transpose this content or that, to communicate this meaning or that, but to highlight the affinity between languages, to show its own possibility" (Derrida, 1985, p. 53).

If the original demands translation, it is understood from the outset that it is not complete in itself, despite its value as an original. The original is also marked by lacks and exists in a dissymmetry even with itself, as it is not governed by the laws of identity. It follows that the translator, like the analyst, if we follow this metaphor of the analyst as translator,

must rescue (*erlösen*), absolve, resolve, seeking to absolve themselves of their own debt, which in the end is the same and has no bottom; 'To rescue in their own language that pure language exiled in the foreign language, to free, transposing it, that pure language captive in the work—this is the translator's task.'

(Derrida, 1985, p. 54)

Thus, in this interplay, language grows. It does not appear as a rigid structure but rather as something fleeting, just as fleeting as the contact between the analysand's utterances and the analyst's interpretation (or perhaps the fleeting nature of interpretation itself—as the point of encounter). Benjamin offers the metaphor of the tangent, which touches the circle at only one diminutive point of meaning, representing the meeting place between the translation and the original, between the analyst and the analysand, and which also enables the movement of that line extending into infinity.

The end of that trajectory, in the same way that one might conceive of a line meeting itself in infinity to form a circle (this is also a promise, despite the specific peculiarities of mathematics in relation to translation), thus fictionally imposes a limit on analysis and translation—but only as an aid to understanding, for in its nature, such a journey never ends. And the fundamental point of this proposed openness—which, in the case of the analytic setting, strips it of the image—is that it does not contradict its unity.

The Death of God and the Language of the Birds

One way of circumventing Babelian confusion seems to have been offered by the language of the birds. Far from situating itself in the universalization of a single language, the language of the birds transcends all language and all translations. It is the very referent of the word in its essence. Beyond the phenomenal materiality of the world, the language of the birds offers no distance between words and things; in a way, the word *is* the thing. It is worth recalling Adam's role in paradise: to name divine creations. What is known about this enigmatic language? According to the traditions that address it—whether mystical, religious, or otherwise—before the babelization of language, the language of the birds was spoken. The renowned alchemist Fulcanelli (1922) stated:

> *Argot* is one of the derived forms of the Language of the Birds, the mother and dean of all others, the language of philosophers and diplomats. It is the one whose knowledge Jesus revealed to his apostles when he sent them his spirit, the Holy Spirit. It is the language that teaches the mystery of things and lifts the veil of the most hidden truths. The ancient Incas called it the Court Language because it was widely used by diplomats, providing them with the key to a double science: sacred science and profane science. In the Middle Ages, it was called Gay Science or Gay Knowledge, the Language of the Gods, and the Divine-Bottle. Tradition asserts that men spoke it before the construction of the Tower of Babel, which caused its perversion and, for most, the complete forgetting of this sacred language.
>
> (p. 53)

It is also said that Tiresias, who experienced femininity and possessed the gift of prophecy, knew the language of the birds, which allowed one to overcome the obstacles of Babelian confusion. This language is supposedly the one Christ taught his apostles, and let us recall that, as Eco (1997) writes, "in Christ there is neither male nor female" (p. 20). This indicates that the relationship between this language and femininity is also present in Christ, as it is in Tiresias. The blind Tiresias knew this language, having been instructed by the goddess Minerva. Fulcanelli (1922) states:

> According to mythology, the famous soothsayer Tiresias had perfect knowledge of the Language of the Birds, taught to him by Minerva, the goddess of Wisdom.

He shared it, they say, with Thales of Miletus, Melampus, and Apollonius of Tyana.

(p. 22).

The words the goddess Athena addresses to the serpent Ericthonius also reso- nate: "Clean Tiresias's ears with your tongue so that he may understand the lan- guage of prophetic birds" (Graves, 1985, p. 10, vol. 2). What Tiresias reveals is this intriguing dimension between translation and femininity. It is precisely his inability to speak of his experience of womanhood, the clumsiness of his words on the sub- ject, that causes him to be struck blind as punishment. Some traditions claim that Saint Francis of Assisi also delved into the mysteries of the language of the birds: "Wait for me here on the path; I am going to preach to my little brothers, the birds" (*The Little Flowers of Saint Francis*, Chapter XVI). Siegfried, the hero of the third part of Wagner's opera *The Ring of the Nibelung*, understands the language of the birds after tasting the blood of the dragon Fafner, whom he has killed with his sword.

The truth-value Benjamin attributes to translation is far removed from align- ing with a metalanguage. Nor is it about assigning the value of a metalanguage to any one language. Heidegger (1955) also did not propose Greek for such a role when he claimed, "In the Greek language, what is said is simultaneously, in an eminent way, that which the said names" (p. 25). This interest can lead to the absurd, as seen in the example Benet (1990) cites from Frazer, who, drawing on Leibniz, notes:

There are as many reasons to believe that Hebrew was the original language of humanity as there are to adopt the opinion of Goropius, who, in his book pub- lished in Antwerp in 1580, sought to demonstrate that the language spoken in Paradise was Dutch. Another writer maintained the thesis that Adam had spoken Basque; while others, going beyond the Scriptures, introduced the confusion of tongues already in Eden, asserting that Adam and Eve spoke Persian, that the serpent spoke Arabic, and that the affable archangel Gabriel conversed with our first parents in Turkish. Another claimed, quite seriously, that the Almighty addressed Adam in Swedish, that Adam responded to his Creator in Danish, and that the serpent tempted Eve in French.

(p. 59)

Thomas More, in his *Utopia*, proposed an artificial universal language, a mix of Hebrew, Greek, and Persian (Matamoros, 1998, p. 5). To Benjamin, the truth- value of a translation does not lie in how faithfully it adheres to the model it origi- nates from, nor in its adequacy to the meaning the original unfolds. The text to be translated does not demand representation; instead, it requires the production of a greater language. Such is the promise embedded in the exercise of translation, which undermines the existence of a divine language. It is precisely this infinite and minuscule point of untranslatability—so distant from the text's essence, akin to Abraham's concept of the core (Derrida, 1997)—that enables the production of other texts: the multiple translations of a single original.

One might think, as Abraham does, about the presence of an unthinkable element within languages, and this is what sparks interest in the paradox of "how to include in a discourse, whatever it may be, that which, by its nature, would escape it by essence?" (Derrida, 1997, p. 73). This is precisely the non-discourse within the discourse, that which eludes the possibilities of translation and representation. The original is not the archetype of others; it is also different from itself, as are the translations of it, despite the relationships between languages. Although Fulcanelli (a name that is itself a translation of Vulcan) asserts that the language of the birds is the *language of the court* (*corte*), in reality, it is a language that does not permit division (*corte*)—that distance which makes possible the production of translations and the creation of a greater language. It is this division that, in Agamben's (2005) words, profanes language—that is, returns it to humans for proper use.

When Nietzsche declares that God is dead, it is understood that the fall of the deity entails the fall of foundations—all foundations, in fact, as it is not about erecting new ones in its place. The tomb of God must remain empty, and anything placed in that void would only repeat the same and not the different. Whether it be atheism, religiosity, philosophy, science, or the body, any pronouncement from opposition, counterculture, or the adversarial current would merely replicate what it rebels against. However, this does not lead to silence. As Derrida affirms, "Nietzsche called for an active forgetting of being: it did not have the metaphysical form Heidegger attributes to it" (1998b, p. 144). While the emptiness of the foundation of being becomes evident, the subject, as fiction, remains a philosophical tool, without implying the resurrection of the dead. The absence of a foundation paves the way for multiplicity, freeing the original from translation as representation in another language. A multivocity of intra- and extra-lingual signifiers emerges.

Thus, at the limits of language, Fulcanelli (1922) concludes his work with the statement: "SILENCE" (p. 206). Milton, in his *Paradise Lost*, asked: "How to recount it, even with the tongue of angels?" Wittgenstein (1973), in his critique of metaphysics, addressed it differently: "Whereof one cannot speak, thereof one must be silent" (p. 183). But it is evident that precisely that which escapes language must be pursued through cracks, through the fractures, encircling it in the shadows where it slips away, and thus, cornered, stealing even a faint fragrance from it—just as the Doppler effect carries, wave-like, the breath and reminiscences of the body that moves away. Translation does not transcend language,

> something real that languages would surround on all sides, like a tower they intend to encircle. No, what they intentionally aim at, each in its own way and all together in translation, is language itself as a Babelian event—a language that is not the universal language in the Leibnizian sense, nor the natural language, since the others still exist. It is the being-language of language, language as such—this unity without any identity with itself, which makes languages exist and makes them languages.
>
> (Derrida, 1985, p. 64)

It presents itself as a harmony among languages and texts, with no aspirations to completeness or totality.

The language of truth for Benjamin distinguishes itself from what would be the *language of the court* or the *language of the birds*. The death of God, as the death of all foundation, is also the death of a universal language. Without an "archetypal language," there is no ultimate referent of meaning for signifiers. Instead, meaning unfolds between words and things. There is no metaphysics of translation. There is no metalanguage. But therein lies the gift, for the multivocity and multiplicity of significations give rise to metaphor, linguistic play, and diversity of meanings.

In the language of psychosis, there appears a use of words that does not allow for these linguistic games and is, therefore, closer to the *"literalness"* to which the language of God, or the language of the birds, or in any case, the language that existed before Babelian confusion would condemn. In Ferenczi's (1932) words, this would lead to stating: "God is mad; the world is in chaos" (p. 227). This opens a relationship between the word as the death of the thing and God as death. God as death is presented in Sgalambro's (1996) words:

> Desiring the good of others is desiring that they do not die, that is all. (How can we reconcile, I repeat, the idea of good with God, who is death itself? I believe, on the contrary, that the idea of God and the idea of death are associated in such a way that we can use either name.)
>
> (p. 116)

Death would then appear as another of God's names or as another of the meanings of the unpronounceable YHWH. The death of God, for its part, would ensure that the word is never silenced.

Originals, as Benjamin tells us, are not rocks or planets; they speak and transform. They do not yield to stasis and are nourished by what speaks of and through them in the proliferation of languages. Continuing with the metaphor of psychosis, that state in which there is no metaphor leads to an encounter with the living dead: "mentally ill people are truly half-dead persons" (Ferenczi letter to Groddeck). It is worth recalling how Beckett—without affirming pathology in him—defended himself against this with the brilliance of his words: "I have always had the impression that there was a murdered being within me. Murdered before my birth. I had to find that murdered being. Try to bring it back to life" (Juliet, 2006).

In Aphorism 125 of *The Gay Science* (2001), titled "The Madman" (or "The Frenzied," depending on the translation), Nietzsche directly addresses for the second time in his work (the first being in "The Prisoners" from *The Wanderer and His Shadow,* 1980) his concept of the death of God. He places the words in the mouth of a madman who approaches a crowd of men who do not believe in God and shouts incessantly, "I am looking for God!" I am looking for God!" The men mock him, and then he reveals to them the nature of the God who has died—and how it was they themselves who killed him, their knife now stained with divine blood. He proceeds to tell them:

> Where is God? I will tell you: we have killed him—you and I. We are all his murderers. But how did we do it? How were we able to drink up the sea? Who gave us the sponge to wipe away the horizon? What did we do when we unchained this earth from its sun? Where is it moving to now? Where are we moving to? Away from all suns? Are we not plunging continually? Backward, sideward, forward, in all directions? Is there still an up or a down? Are we not straying as through an infinite nothing? Does not empty space breathe upon us? Does it not grow colder?
>
> (p. 135)

His words reveal that the pivot and axis of the Earth's rotation are displaced, and the ground is no longer the unalterable rock of solidity. On the contrary, surfaces are revealed as horrifyingly fragile. The place of God has been left empty, vacated; his body decomposes, and the complementary parts of the corruptible world have disappeared along with the dissolution of the Divine beyond, which consolidated the perfect circle offering the security of a flawless mechanism.

So, what to do with the place of God? What to do with that void that has been left? Nietzsche asserts that the tomb of God (which is a tomb because it is the place where the divine corpse lies) must be left empty. He explains how everything that attempts to occupy that space—whether to plug its void or make vain efforts to fill its emptiness—will only revive and repeat what the existence of God represented, thereby preventing us from seeing that killing Him is "the most monumental action" and, perhaps, "Is the greatness of this act too great for us?" (2001, p. 136). Deleuze uses this image to describe what happens with revolutions that, once they seize power, are captured by the apparatus and end up doing exactly the same as what they initially rose against. Active and reactive forces annihilate each other, just as man ceases to be when he kills God; only when he dies in his act of killing is the becoming of the Overman (*Übermensch*) made possible (Deleuze, 1967).

In the matter at hand, the interest lies in the inseverable nature of that space—it is a gap that does not even position itself as such. There is no wound, no scar; it is an open door. If one were to insert a finger into it, one would only know its edges but nothing of the vacuity it contains, which is unintelligible. The non-correspondence of signifiers opens the path for the multiplicity of translations.

Death of God as Death of Representation

The most meaningful dimension to highlight is the death of God as the death of representation. The death of God implies the loss of (ultimate) signifiers. An entire world of absolutes, essences, and transcendental values decomposes with the body of God. The words Nietzsche places in the mouth of the madman speak of the hesitation imposed by facing the place of lack, confronting that for which there are no words and which resides in the reign of the unnamable. It is the world of representation that has fallen. The name of God (Father) is a signifier that does not refer to another signifier but rather to a void; it implies the functioning of a zero, which explains its unnamable nature. When Nietzsche suggests, "Logic is merely the chains of language" (cited by Derrida, *The Supplement of the Copula*, 1998a, p. 216), he states that metaphysics has so deeply infiltrated the architecture of grammatical processes that dispensing with them seems to render thought impossible. For Nietzsche, to think in light of the death of God requires renouncing such structures or accepting them solely as fictions.

The death of God, in turn, touches another edge, another nerve, because, as Freud notes, there is no psychic representation of death. There is also a tangential brushing between Nietzsche and Freud here, even though they do not affirm the same thing. Yet, their discoveries intersect and converge. Freud himself acknowledged this in his *Autobiographical Study* (1925):

> Nietzsche, the other philosopher whose insights and perspectives often coincide in the most surprising way with results laboriously attained by psychoanalysis, I have long avoided precisely because of this; I adhered less to the question of priority than to remaining free from any preconceptions.
>
> (cited by Derrida, 1989, p. 245)

In the relationship between death and silence, Freud (1926) affirms that there is something untransferable in aesthetic, sexual pleasure, and death. The death drive is mute, and thus God dies in silence, with so little commotion that most men remain unaware of it: "When Zarathustra was alone, he said to his heart: Could it be possible? That old saint has not yet heard that God is dead" (Nietzsche, 2003). The possible multiplicity of translations of an original becomes evident in their coexistence. Despite their diversity, contradictions do not necessarily inhabit them. The language of foundations can only find representations or—poor—copies in translations, just as the things of the world were in relation to archetypes (*eidos*). Above all, "translation promises a realm for the reconciliation of languages" (Derrida, 1985, p. 63). This is the messianic promise offered at the end of times by Benjamin. It is an extension to infinity that opens toward the encounter with the other and allows each language to emerge from its cloistered solitude, fostering its own growth in the encounter with another language made possible through translation.

Thus, babelization, far from appearing as a punishment, emerges as a gift that opens the way to encountering difference; it frees us from Paradise, the archetype of sameness, where everything is equal to itself and there is no distance between words and things. "Adam, and above all Eve, have the original merit of freeing us from Paradise; our sin is that we yearn to return to it" (Zuleta, 1980, p. 10). It is known, and not only from psychoanalysis, that the fact that an original does not recognize itself in its translation does not indicate an error in translation, just as the analysand remains implicated in the words they pronounce, even those in which they do not recognize themselves. When Derrida (1997) comments on Abraham's book *The Shell and the Kernel*, he highlights the value of anasemic translation in psychoanalysis, which operates at the boundary between the conscious and the unconscious. Even within the same language—and not just with foreign words—

> the 'same' words that suddenly change meaning, that overflow with meaning and even exceed it, yet remain impassive, identical to themselves, imperturbable, make us read, in the new code of this anasemic translation, what ought to have been read in the other word, the same one, prior to psychoanalysis—this other language that uses the same words by imposing on them a 'radical semantic shift.'
>
> (Derrida, 1997, p. 70)

There may be confusion of tongues within the same language, just as there may be no confusion between different languages.

Language in Analysis

The analysand would understand nothing of themselves if the language imposed is that of the analyst over their own; it would amount to a confusion of tongues. Abraham suggests this in the reading of his book:

> Nothing will be understood unless this text is read as it teaches itself to be read, taking into account the 'scandalous anti-semantics,' that of 'concepts de-signified by virtue of the psychoanalytic context.' This text must be deciphered, then, with the help of the code it proposes and which belongs to its own writing.
>
> (Derrida, 1997, p. 71)

Similarly, the analysand's words present themselves to be read in their own code and with the tools that appear within their discourse. In analysis, more than reading that text constituted by the analysand's words, what is required and demanded is translation: reading them is, from the outset, translating them.

It is desirable that no definitive conclusions have been reached. It is difficult to enjoy the invitation not to understand too quickly. Yet every text, especially the translation of ideas into the grammatical language of sentences ending in periods, demands a certain rigour. It would be better to prefer an ellipsis... But let not the ellipsis mislead. Much has already been insisted upon regarding intra- and trans-textual mutation. Rather, this text is offered, not without its complications, to the nourishment that results from the translation the reader will make of it.

Note

1 A former version of this chapter was published in: Gutiérrez-Peláez, M. (2007). Sobre la traducción y la confusión de lenguas. *Revista Universitaria de Psicoanálisis* (RUP), *7*, 51–69.

Chapter 5

Sándor Ferenczi and Sigmund Freud

On Splitting and Spaltung[1]

Introduction

In psychoanalytic literature, it is most often the case that *splitting* and *Spaltung* are both translated as "splitting" or "scission." This raises a question: are these terms distinct from one another? What kind of relationship exists between them, and is it prudent to use them as equivalents? Clearly, two languages intersect here (three, if we include Spanish), which, in turn, articulate different currents within psychoanalysis, with their convergences and divergences. In the origins of psychoanalytic theory, *Spaltung* refers to Freud, and *splitting* to Ferenczi, as evidenced by their respective writings and the legacy of the latter in the theoretical production of the English school. The relationship between a word and its meaning is by no means immutable; it is always evolving, with new meanings and connotations emerging. This is where it becomes important to question these two concepts (already heavily laden with meaning) and observe what they convey, what particularities they hold, and whether their meaning is diminished when they are fused into a single term.

Splitting is spoken of in many ways, and, in turn, there exists a multitude of terms that seem to refer to it but differ qualitatively both from it and among themselves. Generally, when *splitting* is mentioned in psychoanalytic literature, it refers to Freud's concept of *Spaltung* and not to Ferenczi's contributions regarding it. This is the case in well-known psychoanalytic dictionaries such as those by Laplanche and Pontalis (1997), Roudinesco and Plon (1998), and Hinshelwood (1989), as well as in many contemporary English-language psychoanalytic articles. Ferenczi is not an author commonly cited in literature on *splitting*. In fact, Ferenczi's work is rarely cited in general, which is strange given that it is the most referenced work by Freud throughout his writings (Jiménez Avello, 1998, p. 28). This reflects not only that Ferenczi was a rigorous follower of Freudian theory but also that Freud was a consistent reader of Ferenczi's writings.

Regarding the concepts of *splitting* and *Spaltung*, it could be said—turning to a linguistic twist—that there has been a splitting of the concept of *splitting* itself, as it has lost its own unity. Many terms seek to define it, and, at the same time, many terms are erroneously used as synonyms for it.

DOI: 10.4324/9781003663324-5

In Freud's work, the concept of splitting is not uniform throughout his writings; it shifts and evolves. Within his works, one can find elaborations related to splitting in psychic instances, splitting of representations, and—as appears to have interested him most in the later stages of his work—splitting of the ego, where the representation remains untouched and whole.

It is therefore necessary to review psychoanalytic literature, particularly the works of Freud and Ferenczi, as well as some authors who have commented on their works, to shed light on the meaning of this term and determine if there is an original contribution introduced by Ferenczi. Additionally, it is necessary to examine some aspects of trauma theory as formulated by Ferenczi (contrasting it with Freud's), as *splitting* appears inherent to it. Perhaps the essence of this distinction lies in the divergence between Ferenczi's trauma theory and Freud's.

In reviewing Freud's works, it becomes evident that *Spaltung* appears in both cases of psychosis and neurosis, unlike Ferenczi's conceptualization of *splitting*. Consequently, one could argue that "fragmentation," rather than "splitting" or "scission," is a more appropriate translation for *splitting*.

Splitting and Spaltung: A Question of Terminology

The question arises as to whether these concepts—*splitting* and *Spaltung*—should be used interchangeably. This is especially significant when analyzing the original languages in which these terms were introduced: English for *splitting* and German for *Spaltung*. It is worth considering that Ferenczi himself used the term *splitting* in English, as seen in his "Notes and Fragments" (1932d), among other writings. Given that the legacy of Ferenczi's work has been most strongly preserved within the English school of psychoanalysis (notably due to Balint's stay in London and Ferenczi's own connections to English-speaking psychoanalytic circles, including his relationship with Melanie Klein), the term *splitting* has become anchored in this linguistic context.

Conversely, *Spaltung* is retained in its original German form, as used by Freud. This approach avoids potential confusion that arises when the term "splitting" is used indiscriminately in English, which might otherwise conflate Freud's and Ferenczi's distinct uses of the term. This also circumvents the problem of translating *Spaltung* in Freud and Ferenczi's writings as "splitting" in English—and "*escisión*" in Spanish—creating ambiguity about whether these terms truly align.

Freud's Evolving Use of Spaltung

In Freud's writings, the concept of *Spaltung* does not remain static; it undergoes transformations across different stages of his work. In his early studies, *Spaltung* refers to the splitting of psychic instances, primarily within the context of hysteria, and appears linked to dissociative states. In his later works, Freud applies *Spaltung* to representations and the ego itself, with the splitting of the ego being his most notable exploration of the concept.

For Ferenczi, however, *splitting* appears most clearly in his discussions of trauma. This is particularly evident in his later works, where he examines the impact of traumatic experiences on the psyche, presenting *splitting* as an inherent response to the overwhelming force of trauma. Ferenczi's understanding of *splitting* emphasizes a psychic disintegration that occurs as a desperate strategy for survival, marking a departure from Freud's focus on the coexistence of contradictory attitudes within the ego.

Problem Statement

Scholars of the English school of psychoanalysis often refer to the concept of *splitting* in Ferenczi to explain the mechanisms of fragmentation described by authors from that school. Upon examining translations of these texts into Spanish, one finds that this term often appears as *escisión* ("splitting" or "scission"). Similarly, in psychoanalytic dictionaries (Hinshelwood, 1989; Laplanche & Pontalis, 1997; Roudinesco & Plon, 1998), the term *escisión* directly references Freud's concept of *Spaltung* throughout his work, with no mention of Ferenczi. Furthermore, the term *splitting* does not appear independently in these dictionaries; instead, *escisión*, *splitting*, and *Spaltung* are treated as corresponding translations in Spanish, English, and German, respectively.

In the Laplanche and Pontalis dictionary, two meanings of *escisión* are identified: *escisión del objeto* ("splitting of the object") and *escisión del yo* ("splitting of the ego"). Here, *escisión* is used as a translation for *Spaltung* (*escisión del yo* = *Ichspaltung*) and for *splitting of the ego*; *Objektspaltung* is understood as *splitting of the object* and *escisión del objeto* in Spanish. Differently, the Roudinesco and Plon dictionary prefers the translation *clivaje* ("cleavage") for *Ichspaltung* and *splitting of the ego*, applying the term *escisión* to translate *Trennung* ("scission" or "schism" in English). *Trennung* has a broader range of meanings, not limited to a psychic defence mechanism—for instance, *Trennung* can refer to the "splitting" of a psychoanalytic association. However, they clarify that *escisión* can also refer to *Spaltung*. This is illustrated in Table 5.1.

Table 5.1 Translations of splitting and Spaltung

Dictionary	German	English	Spanish
Laplanche & Pontalis	**Ichspaltung**	Splitting of the ego	Escisión del yo
	Objektspaltung	Splitting of the object	Escisión del objeto
	Spaltung	Splitting	Clivaje
Roudinesco & Plon	**Ichspaltung**	Splitting of the ego	Clivaje (del yo)
	Trennung	Scission or schism	Escisión

Challenges in Translating Ferenczi's Work

Ferenczi's work has not been exempt from the difficulties of translation and the distortion of meanings that occurs when moving between languages. Balint (1969, p. 34), who oversaw much of the English edition of Ferenczi's works, recounts the challenges faced in publishing them, including Jones's refusal to publish Ferenczi's later writings. Regarding the difficulties surrounding the publication of *Confusion of Tongues Between the Adult and the Child* (Ferenczi, 1932a), several studies have explored this issue (Berman, 1995; Blum, 1994; Eyre, 1975; Jacobson, 1994; Modell, 1991; Press, 2006; Rachman, 1989, 1997; Zaslow, 1988).

Even the English editions of Ferenczi's works are not free from complications. As Stanton (1997) notes:

> The last 'edition' of his works in English was undertaken in the 1950s, based on translations mostly carried out around 1920. Unfortunately, many of these translations now appear outdated and inaccurate. The edition is also incomplete, as many early articles written in Hungarian, some German lectures, and the majority of revisions remain untranslated. Furthermore, the work is not chronologically ordered, lacks cross-references, and has not been sufficiently edited to explain the forgotten details of some old debates.
>
> (p. 57)

Stanton himself has worked on revising and correcting these translations by consulting the original German texts.

Translating Ferenczi: The Challenge of Rendering His Work

To trace the origins of the confusion between *splitting* and *Spaltung*, one might hypothesize that this issue arises directly from the effects of translation. The homogenization of the terms *splitting* and *Spaltung* could be attributed to a translational error. However, this is compounded by a series of additional difficulties.

One could attempt to trace Ferenczi's original work in its original language to identify the term he used, which has since been translated into English as *splitting* and in Spanish as *escisión*. The goal would be to determine whether Ferenczi, when writing in German, used the word *Spaltung*, the same term employed by Freud. Unfortunately, access to Ferenczi's original works is far more restricted compared to Freud's, whose texts have been translated directly from the original language with clarifications of terms and concepts, including discussions of their various interpretations.

Ferenczi's work, as translated into Spanish, has often gone through multiple intermediary translations. In many instances, the Spanish editions are based on English translations, and sometimes even on French translations, further complicating efforts to trace the original terminology. For example, the Spanish edition of

Ferenczi's works, published in four volumes under the direction of Dr. José Germain by Espasa-Calpe S.A., follows Balint's English edition. These volumes were translated by Francisco Javier Aguirre from the French edition. The first three volumes were published in 1981, and the fourth in 1984. The French edition itself had been translated, extensively edited, and chronologically ordered by members of the Coq Héron Group, including Judith Dupont, Suzanne Hommel, Françoise Samson, Pierre Sabourin, and Bernard This (*Œuvres Complètes*, 1990–2019, 4 vols.).

As mentioned in a previous chapter, Ferenczi (1932d) was first published in 1985 in French (translated by Judith Dupont) and in Spanish (translated by Beatriz Castillo for Editorial Conjetural), and later in a different edition in Spanish by Amorrortu in 1997 (translated by José Luis Etcheverri and published under the title *Sin simpatía no hay curación.* In 1988, it was published in German and in English for the first time; the latter translated by Michael Balint and published by Harvard Press). This English edition included fragments omitted in the previous publications.

Ferenczi's Language and Its Implications

If it were possible to have full access to Ferenczi's original works, this would not entirely resolve the confusion between terms, even if Ferenczi also used the term *Spaltung*, for it would not necessarily mean he used it in the same way as Freud. Conversely, if Ferenczi used a different term, it would not necessarily imply that he conceptualized something entirely distinct from *Spaltung*. An additional layer of difficulty stems from Ferenczi's own approach to language and terminology. As Balint notes:

> His scientific language… is truly horrifying for any purist or translator. For Ferenczi, words and technical terms were merely—more or less—useful ways of expressing mental experiences.
>
> (Stanton, 1997, p. 66)

Although Ferenczi's native language was Hungarian, most of his works were written in German. However, many of his Hungarian articles remain untranslated into other languages, just as many of his German articles have not been translated into Hungarian, Spanish, or English (Stanton, 1997, p. 203). Stanton has compiled a list of Ferenczi's works that remain untranslated into other languages (pp. 203–214), though as mentioned previously, new publications of his early work are now being compiled, revised and published (Mészáros, Harmatta & Bókay, 2022).

Therefore, a different approach is necessary to clarify the confusion between terms. Recognizing that translation alone cannot resolve this issue, one must instead trace Ferenczi's references to fragmentation mechanisms and psychic defences in his works to isolate the foundation of his concept of *splitting*. This will allow for a clearer understanding of whether Ferenczi's contribution represents a genuinely distinct mechanism compared to Freud's *Spaltung*.

Terminology in Ferenczi's Work: Tracing Splitting and Fragmentation

To explore how Ferenczi's works have been translated, it is pertinent to begin with his 1932 article *Sprachverwirrung zwischen den Erwachsenen und dem Kind*. In Balint's English edition, the article appears under the title *Confusion of Tongues Between the Adult and the Child*. Upon examining the text, one finds that while Ferenczi uses the term *Spaltung*, he does so not to describe the splitting of the ego (as Freud does) but rather the splitting of the personality: *Persönlichkeitsspaltung*, which is translated as "splitting of the personality."

Ferenczi also introduces other terms in this text, marked in italics, such as *Fragmentierung* (fragmentation) and *Atomisierung* (atomization), along with others like *fragmenten* (fragments) and *gespaltet* (split). The following table presents the equivalences of these terms across different languages.

Expanding the Terminology

To fully understand Ferenczi's concept of *splitting*, it is essential to analyze the relationship he establishes between *Persönlichkeitsspaltung* (splitting of the personality) and *Erschütterung* (a term derived from *Schutt*: debris, ruin; meaning "to ruin," "to shake," or "to shock"). These terms are deeply connected to the trauma and its effects on the psyche. Examining other works by Ferenczi in their original language reveals additional insights, as shown in Table 5.2.

Among the German terms Ferenczi uses to describe psychic fragmentation, *Zersplitterung* appears to correspond most closely to the English term *splitting*. In Ferenczi's German writings, one finds the term *Zersplitterung* (*Zersplitterungen* in plural), which etymologically aligns directly with *splitting*. However, there is

Table 5.2 Translations of "Confusion of Tongues Between the Adult and the Child" (1932a)

German (Original)	English (Balint's Translation)	Spanish Translation
Spaltung der Persönlichkeit	Splitting of the personality	División de la personalidad
Spaltung	Splits	Escisión
Psychischen Spaltung	Splitting of the mind	Ruptura psíquica
Gespalten	Split	Dividido
Persönlichkeitsspaltung	Splitting of the personality	División de la personalidad
Die Zahl und die Varietät der Abspaltungen	The number and the various kinds of splits in the personality	El número y la variedad de los fragmentos
Fragmenten	Fragments	(personalidades distintas)
Fragmentierung	Fragmentation	Fragmentación
Atomisierung	Atomization	Atomización

a lack of consistency in how it has been translated. For example, in a letter to Groddeck dated October 10, 1931 (cited by Stanton, 1997), *Zersplitterungen* is translated as "splittings," reflecting a common approach that contributes to the confusion of terms.

Ferenczi also uses the term in *Zum Thema Neokatharsis* (*On the Topic of Neocatharsis*, Bausteine IV, 1985, p. 224). There, however, *Zersplitterung* is translated not as "splitting" but as "disintegration," a choice that more accurately conveys its original meaning. Ferenczi refers to "*seelischen Zersplitterung*," which is correctly rendered as "psychic disintegration." Sabourin (1984) highlights this distinction:

> The fragmentation of the personality (*Zersplitterung*), with its internal division, is merely a particular case, a consequence of hatred and the 'terrorism of suffering.' This concept already foreshadows Winnicott's research on the 'capacity to be alone' and Pancov's work on body image in psychosis.
>
> (p. 14)

Methodology

To achieve the proposed objectives—resolving the conceptual confusion between *splitting* and *Spaltung* and highlighting the originality of Ferenczi's contributions to the former—a conceptual investigation was carried out. This involved a bibliographic review of certain texts and writings by both Freud and Ferenczi, tracing their respective elaborations on these concepts to isolate and emphasize their key features. Additionally, insights from other authors who have contributed to the discussion were incorporated to illuminate the underlying issues.

Despite the difficulties posed by translation, Ferenczi's work was examined in the available materials and versions. From there, the mechanisms of fragmentation he described were traced. This process allowed for the extraction, analysis, and clarification of the unique aspects of the defensive psychic mechanisms he outlined. Finally, these findings were contrasted with Freud's concept of *Spaltung* to clarify the relationship between the two concepts and to delineate the hypothesis with greater precision.

A documentary research approach was used. This included reviewing bibliographic material, hemerographic sources (articles authored by Freud, Ferenczi, and others that address the issues under discussion), and archival materials (such as the Freud-Ferenczi correspondence). Ferenczi's later texts and articles were key to this investigation, as they delve deeply into his conceptualizations of trauma, from which his understanding of *splitting* emerges. For Ferenczi, *splitting* is a defence mechanism that arises in response to trauma. Reviewing his later works allowed the identification of this relationship and its nuances. For an examination of Ferenczi's trauma theory in his late writings, see Gutiérrez-Peláez (2009). To explore his views on war trauma specifically, see Gutiérrez-Peláez (2008b). Freud's texts were equally significant in this study. Following Brook's (1992) framework, Freud's discussions of *Spaltung* were examined at different stages of his work. This enabled the identification of the evolution of Freud's concept and its application to various psychic phenomena, including repression, object splitting, and ego splitting. This comparative analysis between Freud and Ferenczi helped elucidate the conceptual boundaries of *splitting* and its theoretical and clinical implications.

Freud's Concept of Spaltung

Brook (1992), in his article "Freud and Splitting," provides a historical overview of the concept of *Spaltung* in Freud's work and identifies three distinct types of splitting. According to Brook, the first form of splitting to emerge historically was the splitting of psychic instances (1893–1895). Freud linked this to dissociative states and unconscious content that surfaced during states of hypnotic suggestion. Brook argues that this type of splitting laid the foundation for Freud's theorization of repression.

The second type of splitting relates to objects and affects, specifically, the splitting of objects into good and bad. This type is often referred to as the splitting of representations. According to Brook, Freud did not develop this concept extensively; instead, it was later expanded upon by authors such as Kernberg and Klein. Freud's references to this type of splitting can be found in "Instincts and Their Vicissitudes" (2003c), where he suggests that "The original pleasure-ego wants to introject everything good and expel everything bad. Initially, what is bad, foreign to the ego, and external are all identical for it" (p. 254).

Brook also notes an echo of this idea in Freud's later statement from 1923: "No great analytical insight is required to conclude that God and Devil were originally one, a single figure that later split into two opposing entities with contrasting characteristics" (p. 88). In this way, a single representation becomes split, with one part transforming into the opposite of the other.

The third and final type of splitting in Freud's work is the splitting of the ego, which he uses to describe both neurosis and psychosis. This involves the coexistence of two or more contradictory attitudes toward the same event or object. Freud explicitly addresses this phenomenon in "The Splitting of the Ego in the Process of Defense" (1938b), where he restricts the discussion to a case of fetishism. The fetish serves to deny the absence of the female phallus, allowing the child to simultaneously accept and deny what is perceived. This leads to a splitting, as the child both acknowledges and negates what is seen.

In "An Outline of Psychoanalysis" (1938a), Freud extends the concept of ego splitting beyond fetishism. He differentiates between neurosis and psychosis, explaining that in psychoses the denial of reality dominates consciousness and the id operates unchecked. In contrast, neurotics deny reality in their dreams, allowing the id free rein, but during wakefulness, they repress the id and acknowledge reality. Even so, the defence is never entirely successful, as the child retains an awareness of the danger, which manifests as intense anxiety over potential punishment from the father, thus compromising the child's sense of virility.

Freud explains:

> We are probably justified in conjecturing, with universal validity, that in such cases a psychic splitting occurs. Two psychic attitudes are formed instead of a single one: one that accounts for objective reality, the normal one, and another that, under the influence of instinctual drives, detaches the ego from reality. Both coexist side by side.
>
> (p. 203)

Freud adds that if the second attitude prevails, psychosis will ensue. Conversely, if the first attitude dominates, the individual may achieve an apparent recovery from delusion.

Brook's division of *Spaltung* into three stages is far from arbitrary. On the contrary, it underscores foundational psychoanalytic concepts essential for understanding the psyche's structure and operation. The first type of splitting, concerning psychic instances, addresses the origin of the psychic apparatus itself, specifically its establishment through primal repression and the loss of the primal representation. The second type, involving the splitting of representations into good and bad, pertains to the construction of reality. Freud links this to the loss of the object in "Negation" (2003f). The third type of splitting represents another necessary level of division that enables survival. Freud suggests that the ego is inherently split to varying degrees in both neurosis and psychosis. This late formulation of ego splitting, introduced in "The Splitting of the Ego in the Process of Defense" (1938b), is indispensable for understanding the psychic apparatus and its defensive mechanisms.

Divergences Between Splitting and Spaltung

After tracing the respective concepts, we can now examine specific differences and similarities between Freud's *Spaltung* and Ferenczi's *splitting*. To begin, the question arises: why use the term *splitting*? Beyond previous explanations, it is worth noting that Ferenczi himself chose and used this term in his late writings. For instance, in the section "Integration and Splitting" (November 11, 1932), published posthumously in *Notes and Fragments* (2002c). Additionally, he referred to it in a 1930 essay titled *Jeder Anpassung geht ein gehemmter Zersplitterungsversuch voraus* (translated as "Each Adaptation is preceded by an Inhibited Attempt at Splitting"), where he elaborates on disintegration in relation to the death drive, distinguishing it from the life drive, which tends toward reunification of fragmented parts.

The choice of the term *splitting* situates Ferenczi's investigation in dialogue with Freud, highlighting both a shared starting point and the conceptual divergence that followed. The confusion arises partly because *Spaltung* has often been translated as *splitting* in English, fostering the perception of conceptual equivalence where there are substantive differences.

Ferenczi's Use of Terminology

It is evident that while Ferenczi uses the term *Spaltung* in his late writings, he employs it differently than Freud. For Ferenczi, *Spaltung* is consistently used in conjunction with other terms such as *fragmentation, atomization, destruction or annihilation of the self, self-abandonment, collapse, dissolution (Auflösung)*, and *dematerialization (Dematerialisierung)*. In *Confusion of Tongues Between the Adult and the Child* (1932a), Ferenczi introduces *Fragmentation* and *Atomization* as terms belonging to the same conceptual framework, differentiating them only to account for potential acceptance or rejection by the psychoanalytic community or broader audience.

This proliferation of terminology reflects Ferenczi's struggle to capture an experience he observed repeatedly in his clinical work but found difficult to name. The multiplicity of terms serves as a semantic attempt to encircle and articulate the inexpressible. In this sense, Ferenczi's approach to terminology mirrors the psychic fragmentation he describes: breaking into multiple pieces as a means of survival.

While Freud's *Spaltung* involves a coexistence of two opposing attitudes—such as the simultaneous acknowledgement and denial of reality, as seen in fetishism—Ferenczi's *splitting* reflects a much deeper psychic fracture. For Ferenczi, the psyche reacts to trauma by splitting itself in ways that preserve survival but come at a high cost: the loss of unity. The defence entails a psychic abandonment of self, akin to "playing dead" as a last-ditch survival strategy.

Splitting as a Trauma Defence

In Ferenczi's view, *splitting* occurs as a direct response to trauma. The fragmented psyche isolates its parts to prevent total collapse. Ferenczi distinguishes this process from Freud's *Spaltung* by emphasizing the absence of any retained memory of the traumatic event, even in the unconscious. Instead, only the affect remains, leaving the personality fragmented and unable to integrate the experience.

In *Reflections on Trauma* (1984d), Ferenczi suggests that trauma creates an "annihilation of the sense of self," which he likens to the concept of *Erschütterung* ("shock" or "shattering"). This reaction often leads to self-destruction as a defence mechanism. Individuals abandon themselves to the aggressor, internalizing the trauma in ways that paralyze their psychic functioning. Ferenczi observed that such individuals frequently exhibit amnesia for the traumatic event, while the lost fragment of the personality continues to protest internally, manifesting as persistent suffering.

Moreover, Ferenczi's clinical work revealed that the repetition of trauma intensifies fragmentation, resulting in what he termed the *atomization* of the personality. For him, therapeutic work must focus on reuniting these scattered fragments within the analytic setting, offering a space for the patient to re-experience and process the trauma under safe conditions.

Conclusions

Splitting in Ferenczi, as delineated here, represents a novel concept for psychoanalytic theory and differs significantly from Freud's *Spaltung*. It is understood as a defence mechanism whereby the psyche defends itself through its own destruction. The fragmented state allows the individual to cope with the traumatic reality, but at the high cost of losing unity. Such a traumatic situation always arises without the preparation of the person experiencing it.

Ferenczi does use the term *Spaltung*, but in a way distinct from Freud. He does not rely solely on this term but instead employs a range of others that illuminate the meaning he wishes to convey. Whenever Ferenczi employs *Spaltung*, he does so in conjunction with terms such as *fragmentation, atomization, destruction or annihilation of the self, self-abandonment,* and *collapse*. The proliferation of these terms reflects the novelty of what he encountered repeatedly in his clinical practice and the difficulty in capturing it conceptually. When something resists naming, a multitude of terms often arise, as if to encircle the ineffable. Similarly, the process of psychic fragmentation itself involves breaking into multiple pieces as a means of preservation.

Generally, *fragmentation* is regarded as more severe than *splitting*. While trauma can lead to instances of splitting, repeated or intense traumas result in psychic fragmentation. Thus, while *splitting* is a valid translation for *Spaltung*, and indeed aligns with its literal meaning, Ferenczi's trauma theory, particularly in his later writings, more accurately describes *splitting* as *fragmentation*.

For Ferenczi, *splitting* arises as a defence against trauma, differing from Freud's focus on repression or denial (*Verleugnung*). While Freud associated *Spaltung* with the coexistence of two attitudes toward reality, Ferenczi described *splitting* as involving the survival of one part of the psyche at the expense of another, which metaphorically "dies" as a result of the trauma. This psychic splitting is not merely a compartmentalization of conflicting realities; it is a profound psychic disintegration.

In Ferenczi's theory, trauma occurs when a trusted adult becomes an aggressor, destroying the child's sense of safety and paralyzing them with fear. To preserve the pre-trauma state of things, the child identifies with the aggressor, introjecting their qualities to neutralize the external threat. This identification allows the child to maintain the image of the adult as benevolent. However, it also leads the child to internalize the guilt of the aggressor, feeling they deserve punishment for what occurred. The recurrence of trauma increases the fragmentation of the psyche, intensifying the split between fragmented parts of the personality. While some parts strive to reintegrate, others remain cut off, perpetuating a cycle of dissociation. Ferenczi emphasized the necessity of re-experiencing and processing the trauma within the analytic setting to facilitate healing and psychic reintegration.

Freud's *Spaltung* primarily serves to explain mechanisms related to repression, object relations, and the splitting of the ego in both neurosis and psychosis. In contrast, Ferenczi's *splitting* is deeply interwoven with his trauma theory and reflects a psychic defence mechanism unique to extreme trauma. While Freud's concept includes a coexistence of contradictory attitudes, Ferenczi's involves a total fragmentation of the self, with one part often being "lost" to the traumatic experience. This divergence reflects broader theoretical differences between the two analysts. For Freud, the death drive is intrinsic to the psyche, a fundamental force operating from the beginning. Ferenczi, however, viewed the death drive as emerging in response to external trauma, shaped by the failures or actions of the surrounding environment.

Ferenczi's work remains vital to the history of psychoanalysis and provides a lens for understanding both classical and contemporary clinical issues. In recent years, there has been a resurgence of interest in his contributions, particularly in relation to trauma theory and the dynamics of splitting and fragmentation. These developments have highlighted the enduring relevance and richness of Ferenczi's ideas, which offer insights into unresolved issues in psychoanalysis. The significance of Ferenczi's work lies in his clinical and theoretical contributions and in the fundamental problems he identified, which remain central to psychoanalysis today. These issues, rooted in Ferenczi's deep clinical commitment, continue to provoke reflection and dialogue within the contemporary psychoanalytic community.

Note

1 A first version of this chapter was published in: Gutiérrez-Peláez, M. (2010). Diferencias entre los conceptos de *Splitting* en Ferenczi y *Spaltung* en Freud. *Universitas Psychologica*, *9(2)*, 469–484.

Chapter 6

Sándor Ferenczi's Understanding of the Termination of an Analysis[1]

Miguel Gutiérrez-Peláez and Alberto Fergusson

Ferenczi's Radical Approach to Psychoanalysis

Although Freud is the inventor of psychoanalysis, it is Ferenczi who most clearly embodies and inaugurates the desire to carry an analysis to its ultimate conclusion. This is a unique human desire, made possible by the historical and epistemological contingencies of their time: a desire to pursue psychoanalysis to its final consequences, with no retreat before the subject's truth. This desire to reach and face the truth of the unconscious is one we can find throughout Ferenczi's writings. Authors such as Granoff (2004) and Yves Lugrin (2017) suggest that even though Freud is the undoubtable founding father of psychoanalysis, Ferenczi is the first true analyst. They see Ferenczi in a much more radical light than that in which he has been read by certain authors and schools, and closer to how Michael Balint and Jacques Lacan have appreciated: Ferenczi as "the most pertinent of the first-generation authors to question what was required of an analyst, especially in regard to the end of treatment" (Lacan, 1955, cited by Lugrin, 2017).

In "The principle of relaxation and neocatharsis" (1929b), Ferenczi states that "it is essential for the analyst himself to go through an analysis reaching to the very deepest depths and putting him into control of his own character-traits" (p. 124). Ferenczi promoted the analysis of the psychoanalyst, for the lack of analysis of the analyst "can lead to the intolerable situation that our patients are better analysed than ourselves" (Ferenczi, 2012/1932e: 250; see also *Clinical Diary*, 1932c, p. 137), and he believed in the need to carry that analysis to its end.

Lying and the End of Analysis

On September 3, 1927, Ferenczi presented his paper entitled "On the problem of the termination of the analysis" in the 10th *International Psycho-Analytical Congress*, which was held in Innsbruck, Austria. In his lecture, Ferenczi began by addressing a certain clinical difficulty: he had discovered that a patient whom he had been treating for eight months had been lying to him regarding an important financial issue. By lying about this, the patient had failed to follow the basic psychoanalytic principle of communicating to the analyst his true and complete ideas

DOI: 10.4324/9781003663324-6

and associations. Ferenczi had referred to this case in his correspondence with Freud. On August 3, 1926, Ferenczi wrote to his colleague:

> I am writing this time to share with you a small discovery. In a patient who accomplished the feat of forgetting an entire day of his life (and in the process experienced all kinds of things, but mostly 'forbidden' ones on that day), who thus produced one of the otherwise so famous instances of splitting of the personality, I found out that this symptom was an indirect (and unconscious) communication in my direction, to wit, that he had consciously concealed from me or misrepresented to me a whole lot of things. I am convinced that all other instances of this kind can be explained in a similar way – they are an admission of *mendacity*, that is to say, the fact that, in various situations in their lives or in relation to various groups of people, these people expose only parts of their total character and conceal a large part of their behaviour. The cause lies, naturally, in the infantile lie in sexual matters – at the same time, an imitation of the mendacity of adults.
>
> (p. 272)

Continuing with his presentation regarding the end of analysis, Ferenczi asks what is the analyst to do if the pathological aspect of the patient is precisely lying? Ferenczi questions if a patient's mendacity would imply a limit to the psychoanalytic technique, but he refuses to accept this lightly. He refers to a former incident with this patient in which he missed one of his sessions and, the day after, made no mention of his omission. When interrogated by the analyst about this, the patient initially refuses to accept that he has missed his session and only afterwards does he recognize that he has missed it, but has no memory of what he did instead. Through the testimonies of other people, the patient is able to reconstruct the events in which he has spent the day in a state of semi-drunkenness with people strangers to him and of ill repute. Ferenczi concluded that the patient's split personality is a sign of the neurotic mendacity of the patient and evidence of a defect in his character. Therefore, at least in this case, he states, the patient's lying was favourable for the analysis, for it allowed revealing this aspect of the patient's neurotic functioning. Addressing the issues of lying and simulation in neurosis and hysteria, Ferenczi states that: "A real abandonment of mendacity therefore appears to be at least a sign of the approaching end of the analysis" (p. 78).

What is referred to as lies in the adult are in relation to what is mentioned as fantasies in the child. One of the main orientations for the direction of the cure in cases of hysteria has been the unveiling of the fantasies that constitute the patient's psychic reality[2]. But Ferenczi believes it is necessary to reconstruct the patient's reality, differentiating it from the fantasies associated with it. It would require the patient to abandon his tendency to, for example, omit certain events or associations in order to preserve a good image of himself onto the analyst. The paradox which Ferenczi humorously mentions is that the fundamental rule of psychoanalysis can only be fully achieved once the analysis has ended.

Infantile lying, which is used to avoid a perceived greater displeasure as a consequence of honesty, underlies the future development of morality. The passage from a state of amorality to one of morality requires the renunciation of the satisfaction of certain drives. This renunciation and acceptance of certain discontents, speculates Ferenczi, is most probably perceived by the child initially with a feeling of untruth, as a hypocritical act. The analysis must go as deep as to the instinctual foundations that lead to a certain character formation, giving rise to a new and better personality. In this sense, the end of analysis must go beyond a symptom analysis, into a character analysis.

Character Analysis and Subject Transformation

Ferenczi mentions important effects of a completed analysis of a subject. Due to having achieved a separation between his fantasies and reality, the analyzed person has "an almost unlimited inner freedom and simultaneously a much surer grip in acting and making decisions" (p. 81). Following this, he refers to the fact that, in many cases, cured neurotics preserve *tics* and mannerisms despite the resolution of their symptoms and believes that a character analysis must address these issues and, in a sense, put a mirror on the patient's face so he can, for the first time, see the oddities and strangeness of his functioning and even of his physical appearance. This is not directly mentioned by the analyst to the patient, but it is the patient who must become aware of it through his work with the analyst. Ferenczi shows his interest in psychoanalysis not only reaching out to the patient's psyche, but also to his body. This idea of the effect of analysis in the body is what has been more thoroughly developed in his work on "bioanalysis."

Ferenczi refers to the factor of time and believes that an analysis requires having indefinite time available: the more unlimited, the greater the chance for success. But he wisely specifies that more than the time at his disposal, it is the patient's disposition to carry out his analysis with the determination to persist as long as it is necessary. He mentions that abruptly ending an analysis could produce an effect in certain cases, but believes it cannot be recommended as a valid technique, in what appears to be a reference (and a distance) from Freud's analysis of Sergei Pankejeff (known as the "Wolf Man"). In an analysis, the whole array of the patient's memories, repetitions and "working through" are displayed. Transference and the overall patient-analyst relation are crucial; on the side of the patient, regarding his dependence and mistrust of the analyst, and on the side of the analyst, the importance of sincerity, of recognizing his mistakes and not responding to the patient's attitude from his own intrinsic, unresolved, dispositions. This is why Ferenczi insists on the need for the analyst to be completely analyzed. Ferenczi mentions that he does not find structural differences between "so-called" training analysis and therapeutic analysis. He believes it is not enough with a one-year analysis for the analyst: he has to have undertaken a complete analysis of his unconscious.

"The proper ending of an analysis," says Ferenczi, "is when neither the physician nor the patient puts an end to it, but when it dies of exhaustion, so to speak"

(p. 85). We will go back to this assertion. Regarding the transference with the analyst, it falls as well at the end of analysis: "A truly cured patient frees himself from analysis slowly but surely" (p. 85). Later, in his *Clinical Diary* (1932), Ferenczi mentions that the end of analysis implies the emancipation of the patient from the analyst. Ferenczi also mentions that it is common to find symptom transformations towards the end of analysis; for example, a hysteric presenting obsessive ideas, conversion symptoms in obsessional intellectuality, and even temporary psychosis in neurotic patients.

In this ground-breaking paper, Ferenczi presents ideas regarding the ending of analysis that are pertinent for present times. He believes that there could be an end to an analysis (we will see later in what sense an analysis is interminable), that there may be a logical end to them and that many times the causes of an analysis not reaching an end lie in the insufficient analysis of the analyst and his incapacity to see and recognize the weak points of his own personality.

The Concept of Termination

Going back to his remark according to which "The proper ending of an analysis is when neither the physician nor the patient puts an end to it, but when it dies of exhaustion, so to speak" (p. 85), it is worth highlighting that the German term that Ferenczi uses for termination is *Erschöpfung*. Its etymology is the noun of the verb *erschöpfen*, and this, in turn, is a derivation of *"er"* + *"schöpfen."* *Schöpfen* can be used as drawing out (a liquid) or taking in (air). Because of this, with the prefix *"er,"* it implies taking out or removing completely, that is, "exhausting." Therefore, "exhaustion" is a correct translation of the word, but it is worth specifying its polyvalence, beyond its common use as a state of severe fatigue. *Erschöpfung* refers to "exhaustion" also in the sense of exhausting completely an existing source, for example, natural resources such as the precious rocks available in a mine. Once the resources have been extracted completely, there is nothing else to retrieve from that source. Ferenczi makes it clear that what is "exhausted" is not the analyst or the analysand, but the analysis itself. It is the moment when we can say there is no more unconscious material available for extraction.

But *Erschöpfung* allows an even deeper level of understanding. The word *Schöpfen*, present in *Erschöpfung*, refers to a creation, in the sense of an artistic, very formal creation (as used, for example, in Friedrich Hölderlin's "Mnemosyne" and in Martin Heidegger's "The Origin of the Work of Art"). *Schöpfen* is also the creator, as in the "Creator of all things," or as in the Creator (*Schöpfer*) and the creature/created (*Geschöpf*). In a highly ceremonial sense, one would also speak of an artist as a creator (*Schöpfer*), implying the creation of something truly original. Accordingly, what can be found at the end of an analysis, in the termination of its experience, is not only the exhaustion of the experience of the unconscious, but an absolutely original creation on behalf of the subject. This creation is not something that is elaborated *ex Nihilo* or "out of the blue," but precisely a remnant once the reduction of the unconscious through the analysis has isolated that singular formation of the subject that can allow him a new relation with his reality and with his own psyche. This differs from Freud's understanding of the end of analysis as presented in his 1937 text "Analysis Terminable and Interminable." It aligns more closely with Jacques Lacan's later elaborations, in which analysis is conceived as the isolation of the incurable dimension of the subject. Central to this perspective is Lacan's concept of the sinthome—the element that is rediscovered at the end of analysis. The sinthome is intimately linked to the subject's singularity: it is the result of unconscious decisions, desires, and historical contingencies, a true event of the body. This transformation becomes the defining mark of the subject's relation to his own existence.

Ethics and the Analyst's Self-Analysis

On many occasions, Ferenczi insists on the importance of the analysis of the analyst (Fergusson, 2015, p. 192). The three main pillars of psychoanalytic training (psychoanalysis of the analyst, clinical supervision and study of the psychoanalytic theories and doctrine) are a Ferenczian contribution that still exists today and that are a common ground in all psychoanalytic associations and schools, despite the important differences present amongst them. As he writes in "Confusion of tongues between the adult and the child" (1933b):

> This leads to the side issue—the analysis of the analyst—which is becoming more and more important. Do not let us forget that the deep-reaching analysis of a neurosis needs many years, while the average training analysis lasts only a few months, or at most, one to one and a half years. This may lead to an impossible situation, namely, that our patients gradually become better analysed than we ourselves are, which means that although they may show signs of such superiority, they are unable to express it in words; indeed, they deteriorate into an extreme submissiveness obviously because of this inability or because of a fear of occasioning displeasure in us by their criticism.
>
> (p. 158)

Ferenczi also believed that psychoanalysis had the power to awaken people and, in that sense, moved in a direction contrary to that of hypnosis. While hypnosis involves the effect of language on the psychic apparatus in the form of a command issued by an Other—one that remains unconscious to the subject— psychoanalysis aims to awaken the subject to those commands of the Other that he has mistaken for his own will, and which he unknowingly obeys through his actions, unaware that he is enacting the will of another. This is conceiving psychoanalyzing as "dehypnotizing," as he wrote in his *Clinical Diary* (1932d, p. 62).

In 1981, Ferenczi wrote a very impressive letter[3] that, due to its richness and complexity, is worth transcribing completely. The communication is directed to

Frédéric Karinthy (1887–1938), a journalist of his time who initially was quite fond of psychoanalysis, but who subsequently lost interest in it. Ferenczi writes:

> My dear Karinthy ... You said that you knew two types of wise man and two types of science. The first searches for the truth and strives to awaken a sleepy humanity; the second one avoids by all means disturbing the quietude of the drowsy world and even tends to make it fall into a deeper slumber. Psychoanalysis, you said, possesses that special ability to awaken us, trying to give the human psyche, by means of knowledge, not only command over oneself but also of our organic and physical strengths.
>
> But now you write that it is necessary to stop being in analysis in order to preferably study those who speak of peace, harmony, welfare, and that, with the help of clever suggestions, including hypnotic dreams, surreptitiously introduce in the human psyche sensations, ideas and reasonable, intelligent, comforting and joyful intentions.
>
> I have previously found your words regarding the power of the wiseman somewhat audacious, but since then I have been able to convince myself of their certainty. I recognized in principle the ability of "awakener" which corresponded to psychoanalysis and I have not changed my mind, because I am convinced that without an authentic and brave science, any effort to find happiness is useless and at best can only arouse a temporary illusion. But you, on the contrary, have apparently lost patience (possibly due to present miseries); you neither wish the truth nor science and only aspire to find a bit of joy for our tormented world at any price, even if it means lulling it to sleep. In a word, I would simply wish to acknowledge here that, of us two, I am now the one who has not abandoned the ranks of those who awaken.

There is a difference, for Ferenczi, between a science that "lulls" and a science that "awakens." This awakening power of psychoanalysis was present in his first psychoanalytic writings and prevailed throughout his work. This was what he believed to be the true power of psychoanalysis and what gave it its potentiality to change not only the individual's psychic suffering, but to change society itself. If the analysts are the ones carrying out these fundamental processes, the need for them to carry out their own analysis to its end is certainly much more imperative. It is a Ferenczian legacy that the ethics of the analyst implies not retreating in his desire to delve as deep as he can into his own unconscious.

Conclusion

Sándor Ferenczi's exploration of the end of analysis reveals his profound commitment to the transformative potential of psychoanalysis. By emphasizing the necessity of confronting the deepest layers of the unconscious and fostering an original creation at the conclusion of treatment, Ferenczi offers a vision of psychoanalysis as a deeply ethical and emancipatory practice. His insistence on the analyst's self-analysis underscores the importance of the ethical responsibility of the analyst, ensuring that they do not impose their own unresolved issues onto their patients. Ferenczi's pioneering ideas about termination, character transformation, and the interplay between fantasy and reality continue to be key issues in contemporary psychoanalytic practice and training.

Notes

1 Some of the ideas presented in this chapter were presented in the book: Fergusson, A., & Gutiérrez-Peláez, M. (2022). The end of analysis [pp. 60–67]. In: *Sándor Ferenczi. A contemporary introduction.* London, UK: Routledge.
2 This inevitably evokes Lacan's proposal of the end of analysis as a "*traversée du fansasme.*"
3 Letter we referred to in Chapter 4.

Chapter 7

Ferenczi's Unique Trauma Theory[1]

Introduction

It is relevant to reflect on the reasons why, in the last years of his life and career, Ferenczi came to write and produce so much material on the theory of trauma and on therapeutic practice in relation to trauma. According to Dupont (1998): "Ferenczi constructed his theory of trauma [...] gradually, on the basis of clinical observations" (p. 236). His final contributions (as they are called in the title of Balint's compilation) differ from his earlier works both formally and in terms of the interests that gave rise to them. The basic unity displayed by the content of the texts dating from those years fully justifies Balint's presentation of them as a single volume entitled *Final Contributions to the Problems and Methods of Psychoanalysis* (Ferenczi, 1955e). Each of Ferenczi's last writings departs further than its predecessor from Freud's ideas, and it is because of these differences that they are most original. It is precisely this part of his oeuvre that attracted the most criticism.

Ferenczi's *Clinical Diary* (Dupont, 1985) and some of the *Notes and Fragments* (1930–1932) illustrate his developing ideas on trauma and the psychic mechanisms involved in it, rather than presenting finished theories. Trauma is portrayed as something that occurs in the adult-child encounter and directly influences the construction of the subject's narcissism.

Trauma According to Confusion of Tongues between Adults and the Child (1932a)

In "Confusion of tongues between adults and the child," Ferenczi (1932a) expands on the idea of the external origin of trauma and its effects in terms of character and neurosis; he reconsiders the role of the traumatic factor—which has, in his view, been set aside in psychoanalytic theory—and returns to some earlier Freudian formulations. He distinguishes two kinds of love which are here involved, the tender and the erotic current; he holds that a child is pervaded psychically, affectively and biologically by the former, while the latter is (in most cases) the exclusive province of adulthood. However, some adults predisposed to psychopathology confuse the tender language of the child with the sexual desires of a mature person and allow

DOI: 10.4324/9781003663324-7

themselves to be carried away by these with no heed for the consequences. This is precisely what the title implies, suggesting the confusion of tongues occurring in the adult in relation to what the child is expressing. The child cannot always defend himself or demonstrate his rejection because he is paralyzed by intense fear. More specifically:

> The same anxiety, however, if it reaches a certain maximum, compels them to subordinate themselves like automata to the will of the aggressor, to divine each one of his desires and to gratify these; completely oblivious of themselves they identify themselves with the aggressor. Through the identification, or let us say, introjection of the aggressor, he disappears as part of the external reality, and becomes intra- instead of extra-psychic; [...] the attack as a rigid external reality ceases to exist and in the traumatic trance the child succeeds in maintaining the previous situation of tenderness.
>
> (Ferenczi, 1932a, p. 162)

In this way, the child introjects the adult's sense of guilt. What previously seemed like a game to the child, behind the sexual act or sexual abuse perpetrated by the adult, is transformed into something for which the child deserves to be punished. The child's successful recovery from this aggression, however, means that he has already effected a split, being both guilty and innocent, destroying the links with his own feelings, perceptions and sensations, and sinking into a confusional state. So, the child does not defend himself, but identifies with the aggressor and introjects what appears to him to be threatening. The child's reaction thus foreshadows the split in his personality. Elsewhere, Ferenczi (1929a) develops the idea that the child confronts intense fear if his genital sensations are aroused prematurely, as his wishes are on the level not of an adult's violent passion but of play and tender affective manifestations.

Ferenczi distinguishes three potentially traumatic situations: incestuous seductions, passionate punishment and the terrorism of suffering. As a result of the trauma: "the psychic apparatus has split: whereas a part of the child has recorded the experience, there is another part that splits off and seeks to maintain the belief that 'nothing has happened'" (Genovés, in Jiménez Avello, 1998, p. 262, translated). In other words, such patients exhibit both a passive resistance to the attacks inflicted on them by the environment and a splitting of their being into a suffering, lacerated part on the one hand and a part which has made itself totally insensitive but knows everything. This idea was expressed clearly by Ferenczi (1931a) in "Child-analysis in the analysis of adults":

> It really seems as though, under the stress of imminent danger, part of the self splits off and becomes a psychic instance observing and desiring to help the self, and that possibly this happens in early – even the very earliest – childhood.
>
> (p. 136)

The trauma has the effect that the child lacks mechanisms for binding the excess excitation. Ferenczi regards the traumatic factor as universal and holds that until this material is reached—it is initially accessible only through repetition and not through remembering—an analysis cannot be deemed to be finished.

Towards the end of "Confusion of tongues between adults and the child," Ferenczi attempts a more precise outline of the psychic consequences of the experience of trauma. He writes:

> If the shocks increase in number during the development of the child, the number and the various kinds of splits in the personality also increase, and soon it becomes extremely difficult to maintain contact without confusion with all the fragments, each of which behaves as a separate personality yet does not know even the existence of the others. Eventually it may arrive at a state which – continuing the picture of fragmentation – one would be justified in calling atomization. One must possess a good deal of optimism not to lose courage when facing such a state, though I hope even here to be able to find threads that can link up the various parts.
>
> (Ferenczi, 1932a, p. 165)

This passage throws even more light on the picture encountered by Ferenczi as he contemplates the material brought by his patients. The defence may give rise to a division of the psyche into a number of parts according to the impact and intensity of the traumas to which the child is exposed. He suggests the term atomization [*Atomisierung*], undertaken as a precaution against another manifestation, fragmentation [*Fragmentierung*], which, however, appears to correspond more to the clinical evidence. Here, one can observe how this idea is progressively taking shape in his writings.

The adult uses the child for the satisfaction of his drives, whether sexual or emotional (anger or hate). The adult's act takes the child by surprise and leaves him defenceless. The traumatic event destroys the child's prior state of security with respect to himself and the world about him: someone who was formerly the bearer of feelings of trust for the child now removes him from his state of security and plunges him into one of total helplessness, so that the subject is traumatized and overcome instead by absolute insecurity. In consequence, he submits and identifies with the aggressor. He thereby causes the aggression itself to disappear from external reality and maintains the tender situation that prevailed before the trauma, which bursts into and smashes the old order of the psychic constitution. However, Ferenczi also tells us that this in itself is not enough to produce trauma; as in Freud's ideas on the origins of trauma, a second element is also required, which in this case is the adult's response. In Ferenczi's view, there are two stages in the pathologization of trauma; that is to say, the traumatic situation by itself does not necessarily result in the generation of trauma. There is a second phase, which has to do with the lack of support from the persons—in particular, the mother—on whom the child depends (Dupont, 1998). With regard to this second phase, it is pointed out that: "The mother's disapproval as a dysfunction of language is a traumatic agent that redoubles the early beginnings, which are dysfunctions of the child's libido" (Sabourin, 1984, p. 19, translated). This behaviour by adults towards the abused child bears a direct relationship to the psychic mechanism involved in the crystallization of the trauma.

Trauma and Remembering

Ferenczi's trauma theory, as outlined above, assumes additional complexity in regard to how the effects of—and on—memory and remembering should be conceived. The reaction that gives rise to the trauma is the break with reality, which results in the self-destruction of consciousness. A stoppage of thought and perception occurs, paralyzing the functions of the psyche, and the impressions concerned go unrecorded, even at the unconscious level. In consequence, there will be no way of remembering what has happened. The psychic apparatus does not store any of these traumatic impressions. The outcome is a 'split in the personality,' which locates them pretraumatically, denying that anything has happened, and the attitude of the adult who pretends that nothing has happened forces the subject to forget, preventing any possibility of working through and making for disavowal. Since nothing has been recorded, so that there is no possibility of remembering or of accession of material to consciousness, what is involved plainly has nothing to do with repression.

Ferenczi notes that:

> This generally involves a trauma suffered in early childhood, which has never been experienced consciously and therefore cannot be remembered. He presents trauma as a concussion, producing a split in the personality. In order to illustrate this split, he uses a whole series of images: splitting off of a dead part, killed by the violence of the shock, enabling thus the rest to live a normal life, but with part of the personality missing and out of reach, like a sort of cyst inside the personality; or multiple splits under the effect of repeated shocks which may go as far as atomisation: the personality fragments in order to present a larger surface area to the shock

> (Dupont, 1998, p. 235)

The trauma appears to be unforeseen. The subject reacts with what Ferenczi calls a 'fleeting psychosis,' a break with reality. This psychotic split paralyzes all psychic activity. Motility becomes impossible, perception is blocked, and so is the activity of thought, inhibiting resistance and inducing a state of passivity: "The subject becomes malleable and reacts with fragmentation or even atomization of the personality" (Dupont, 1998, p. 236).

By this identification with the person responsible for the aggression, the psyche guarantees its own existence. It thereby finds a way of surviving the ill-treatment. In addition, it succeeds in preserving the 'good' image of the adult. These types of aggression are serious; they are like rapes or passionate punishments—in particular, punishments for misdeeds the child does not think he has committed. Although he does not consider them to be his own, the child finds it necessary to identify with the aggressor in order to maintain this good image, which is of fundamental importance to him. By virtue of the split, he becomes a child who is at one and the same time innocent and guilty. The adult, for his part—prompted either by his guilt or by the pressing need to avoid the consequences of his act—denies the facts, and this intensifies the effects of the trauma and causes the child to distrust his own feelings.

In some of the posthumously published *Notes and Fragments* (1930–1932), Ferenczi spells out the effects of trauma on the psyche. For instance:

> 'Shock' = annihilation of self-regard – of the ability to put up a resistance, and to act and think in defence of one's own self; perhaps even the organs which secure self-preservation give up their function or reduce it to a minimum. (The word *Erschütterung* is derived from schütten, i.e. to become 'unfest, unsolid', to lose one's own form and to adopt easily and without resistance, an imposed form ['like a sack of flour'].)
>
> (Ferenczi, 1932b, pp. 253–254)

Self-abandonment is the person's response to the traumatic situation. Subjectivity lies in ruins, and the person is destroyed, having totally surrendered to the 'other' who perpetrated the aggression.

It can be seen that the 'shock' to which Ferenczi refers has the particular feature that it always occurs when the victim is unprepared. Having previously been pervaded by a sense of security, the child then loses trust in himself and the world, either partially or completely. The unpleasure to which this psychic shock gives rise proves impossible to overcome; in other words, the child is unable to deploy a defence that will act on the world about him (i.e., alloplastically) and thereby eliminate the cause of the suffering, nor can he produce a representation matching the suffering whereby some kind of working through or processing might be possible. The trauma immediately results in an overflowing of anxiety in the form of a sense of helplessness that stands in the way of any positive reaction to the situation, such as fight or flight in relation to the external danger.

Hence:

> Unpleasure increases and demands 'outlet'. Self-destruction as releasing some anxiety is preferred to silent toleration. Easiest to destroy in ourselves is the cs – the integration of mental images into a unit [...]. Disorientation [...]
>
> (Ferenczi, 1931b, p. 249)

Ferenczi notes that an unexpected traumatic situation can have a certain anaesthetic effect, which he sees as the complete or partial cessation of psychic activity and the generation of a state of passivity that precludes resistance of any kind.

Motility, perception, and thought come to a halt. By virtue of this loss of perception, the personality finds itself totally unprotected.

The outcome is a form of psychic paralysis with the following consequences:

1 the course of sensory paralysis becomes and remains permanently interrupted;
2 while the sensory paralysis lasts, every mechanical and mental impression is taken up without any resistance; and
3 no memory traces of such impressions remain, even in the unconscious, and thus the causes of the trauma cannot be recalled from memory traces.

(Ferenczi, 1931b, p. 240)

To gain access to these causes, Ferenczi thinks it necessary to repeat the trauma in benign, more favourable circumstances, so that it can, in this way, be perceived by the subject for the first time and thereby find a channel for motor discharge. Ferenczi's keen interpretation and theorization of trauma differ significantly from Freud's first trauma theory and presents ideas that enrich our understanding of the symptoms and suffering of traumatized patients as insistently manifested in clinical consultations.

Conflicts between Freud and Ferenczi Over Ferenczi's Trauma Theory

While bearing in mind the foregoing considerations, let us now go back a little and take another look at the reasons for Freud's negative reaction to the presentation of Ferenczi's paper "Confusion of tongues between adults and the child" (1932a). What was it in Freud's conception of trauma and psychic reality in 1932 that made the ideas expressed by Ferenczi in that contribution so unacceptable to him? Did the notion of 'reality' account fully for the dispute, or was there something more?

That paper by Ferenczi was the opening contribution at the XIIth Congress of Psychoanalysis, held in Wiesbaden, Germany, on September 12, 1932. Ferenczi presented it to an audience of psychoanalysts who were active at the time, not, however, including Freud, who did not attend owing apparently to ill health. Although Freud did not hear the presentation, he was familiar with it from Ferenczi's own mouth, Ferenczi having read it to him at his home some time before. Freud's response was devastating: he instantly rejected it. Dupont describes what happened as follows:

Ferenczi stopped off at Vienna to read Freud the paper he was to present at the Congress, 'Confusion of Tongues between Adults and the Child'. It was a painful encounter, in which mutual incomprehension between the two men came to a head. Freud, deeply shocked by the contents of the paper, demanded that Ferenczi refrain from publishing anything until he had reconsidered the position he put forth in it.

(Dupont, 1985, pp. xvi–xvii)

Ferenczi gave his lecture nevertheless, but was most dismayed by this contre-temps, as his letters to Freud (in Falzeder & Brabant, 2000, pp. 442–443) and Grod-deck (in Ferenczi & Groddeck, 2002) suggest. Among the analysts who did hear the presentation at the Congress were "Anna Freud, Federn, Alexander, Jekels, Jones, de Groot, Brunswick, Simmel, Hárnick, Bonaparte, Sterba, Reik, Balint, Deutsch, Rado, Weiss, Odier, Glover, Roheim, Menninger, de Saussure" (Mas-son, 1984, p. 151). The rejection of the paper was general, the discontent to which it gave rise being attributed to the new methods presented, the implications of a return to the seduction theory, the focus on infantile sexual abuse, the emphasis on working with difficult cases, and the manifest break with Freud's thought. Yet this was not the beginning of the Freud-Ferenczi conflict, which can probably be traced back to the publication of *The Development of Psychoanalysis*, published jointly by Ferenczi and Rank in 1924 (Ferenczi & Rank, 1924).

On the other hand, it is odd that this 1932 contribution in particular should have caused such a stir, because, even if it marks an important turning point in Ferenczi's work, it is not inconsistent with the trend of the rest of his oeuvre. Starting with his pre-analytic writings, Ferenczi had expressed his interest in difficult cases and presented unorthodox ideas on psychiatry and technical innovations for the treat-ment of his patients, all prior to the commencement of his relationship with Freud.

Many of the commentators on the dispute between Freud and Ferenczi over "Confusion of tongues between adults and the child" concentrate on elements of countertransference between the two analysts. However, with regard to Freud's rejection of Ferenczi's contribution, the point most authors emphasize is surely the return to Freud's first theory of neurosis. It is considered that Freud's trauma theory, which featured in his early writings and held sway until he developed his concept of psychical reality, had been left behind by Freud's later formulations. Ferenczi thus seemed to be reviving and putting forward conceptions that had been superseded by psychoanalysis at the very beginning of the century. The fact that Ferenczi, too, was to some extent aware of the presence of such elements in his thought is suggested by his letter to Freud of July 20, 1930:

> Somewhat more prematurely than you, Herr Professor, but I, too, am occupying myself greatly with the problem of death, naturally, likewise in connection with my own fate and its chances for the future. A part of my bodily self-love seems to have sublimated itself into scientific interest, and this subjective factor has sensitized me, I believe, to psychic and other processes in our neurotics, which are playing themselves out in moments of real or supposed lethal danger. That was certainly the way in which I came to freshen up the apparently antiquated (at least temporarily cast- aside) trauma theory.
>
> (Falzeder & Brabant, 2000, p. 396)

Tellingly, Freud was not scandalized by this letter—so it is not at all clear that the ideas advanced in Ferenczi's paper were in fact dismissed out of hand by Freud. Indeed, as will be shown below, Freud himself continued to adduce these notions in his writings and lectures subsequent to the supposed abandonment of the seduction theory.

As we know, before 1897, Freud had developed a theory of the aetiology of neurosis that included hereditary factors, concomitant circumstances and specific causes, among these last being active seductions of infants by adults. Subsequently, as he recounts in *On the history of the psycho-analytic movement*, he abandoned this theory in favour of the concept of psychical reality. He writes:

> Influenced by Charcot's view of the traumatic origin of hysteria, one was readily inclined to accept as true and aetiologically significant the statements made by patients in which they ascribed their symptoms to passive sexual experiences in the first years of childhood – to put it bluntly, to seduction. When this aetiology broke down under the weight of its own improbability and contradiction in definitely ascertainable circumstances, the result at first was helpless bewilderment. Analysis had led back to these infantile sexual traumas by the right path, and yet they were not true. The firm ground of reality was gone. [...] [However, if] hysterical subjects trace back their symptoms to traumas that are fictitious, then the new fact which emerges is precisely that they create such scenes in phantasy, and this psychical reality requires to be taken into account alongside practical reality. This reflection was soon followed by the discovery that these phantasies were intended to cover up the auto-erotic activity of the first years of childhood, to embellish it and raise it to a higher plane. And now, from behind the phantasies, the whole range of a child's sexual life came to light.
>
> (Freud, 1914, pp. 17–18)

For Ferenczi, Freud's discovery that his female neurotic patients lied was catastrophic:

> According to Ferenczi, Freud, who initially followed Breuer with great enthusiasm, has been irremediably disappointed by the discovery that hysterics lie. Since then he no longer loves his patients. He again becomes a materialistic, scientific investigator (entry of 1 May) emotionally detached from psychoanalysis, which he approaches henceforth on a purely intellectual level.
>
> (Dupont, 1985, p. xxiv)

Ferenczi's commentators readily assert that Freud abandoned the traumatic seduction theory before 1900, but his subsequent references to it are, at any rate, then omitted. Yet it is insufficient to argue that Freud's dismissal was attributable to Ferenczi's revival of his own early seduction theory. After all, on the one hand, a detailed reading of Ferenczi's contributions from this period—in particular, his Wiesbaden paper—clearly indicates that Ferenczi was producing other things (as the previous paragraph and the next one show), and, on the other, Freud's writings reflect the vicissitudes of his understanding of the objective reality involved in traumatic experiences. It is therefore important to review the most significant occasions when Freud returns to the effect of objective reality on the production of trauma.

The most decisive passage is to be found in *From the history of an infantile neurosis* ('Wolf Man') (Freud, 1918), where Freud writes:

> I must here turn for a moment to the history of the treatment. When once the Grusha scene had been assimilated – the first experience that he could really remember, and one which he had remembered without any conjectures or intervention on my part – the problem of the treatment had every appearance of having been solved. From that time forward there were no more resistances; all that remained to be done was to collect and to co-ordinate. The old trauma theory of the neuroses, which was after all built up upon impressions gained from psychoanalytic practice, had suddenly come to the front once more.
>
> (pp. 94–95)

According to Sabourin, at times Freud seems to reject any revisiting of the old trauma theory (as in the case of Schreber), whereas elsewhere he does apparently return to it, as "for example in 1924 when he confirms that seduction 'retains a certain aetiological importance, and even to-day I think some of these psychological comments are to the point'" (Sabourin, 1984, p. 17, translated). Sabourin is referring to a footnote added by Freud in 1924 to his 1896 text "Further remarks on the neuropsychoses of defence," in which Freud treats seduction as a concrete act and not as a phantasy or masquerade. The 1924 footnote reads:

> This section is dominated by an error which I have since repeatedly acknowledged and corrected. At that time I was not yet able to distinguish between my patients' phantasies about their childhood years and their real recollections. As a result, I attributed to the aetiological factor of seduction a significance and universality which it does not possess. When this error had been overcome, it became possible to obtain an insight into the spontaneous manifestations of the sexuality of children which I described in my "Three Essays on the Theory of Sexuality" (1905). Nevertheless, we need not reject everything written in the text above. Seduction retains a certain aetiological importance, and even to-day I think some of these psychological comments are to the point.
>
> Freud (2003d)

This shows that Freud did not adopt a definitive position vis-à-vis the seduction theory. Furthermore,

> in some of the letters to Fliess, censored by Freud's official followers, Max Schur found details that help us to understand the magnitude of Freud's conflict in this connection. Unlike his successors, Freud never inclined towards definitive opinions for or against the seduction theory.
>
> (Sabourin, 1984, p. 15, translated)

Although the existence of this dispute about the reality of a trauma is not in doubt, the old trauma theory is seen not to be conceptually abandoned by Freud— far from it. Hence, there must necessarily be 'something more' in Ferenczi's 1932 text that aroused Freud's ire. There is indeed a less noticed aspect of the Freud-Ferenczi polemic about Confusion of tongues, which has to do with the drive element, and which could be expressed as follows: whereas for Freud there is a deadly component in every subject, for Ferenczi this component is attributable to the 'other'; it comes about owing to the traumatic effect of the other's action, and if this were not the case there would, in his view, be no reason for it to be unleashed.

However, on this point too, Freud presents different ideas at different times. At the end of the *Three Essays on the Theory of Sexuality* (Freud, 1905, p. 234), he writes: "The external influences of seduction are capable of provoking interruptions of the latency period or even its cessation, and [...] in this connection the sexual instinct of children proves in fact to be polymorphously per- verse". (This passage is quoted by Sabourin, 1984, p. 14.) External traumatic factors, such as adult seduction of infants, can have catastrophic effects on the development of the libido, holding it back, delaying it, or diverting it into other channels.

In a footnote to *The Ego and the Id* (1923), Freud writes:

> The battle with the obstacle of an unconscious sense of guilt is not made easy for the analyst. Nothing can be done against it directly, and nothing indirectly but the slow procedure of unmasking its unconscious repressed roots, and of thus gradually changing it into a conscious sense of guilt. [...] it must be honestly confessed that here we have another limitation to the effectiveness of analysis; after all, analysis does not set out to make pathological reactions impossible, but to give the patient's ego freedom to decide one way or the other.
>
> (p. 50)

Freud here comes up against a barrier to psychoanalysis—a point beyond which it is impossible to advance further. The unconscious sense of guilt is for him a deadly aspect of the death drive that has always been present and cannot be eliminated by psychoanalysis.

When Ferenczi discusses the death drive, he links it to the concept of guilt, a concept on which both Ferenczi and Freud wrote at length:

> The notion of the traumatolytic function of dreams, which proved so useful for understanding repetitive dreams, [was] an original idea of Freud's that was further developed by Ferenczi and reinstated by the master in 1931 in the first of his New Introductory Lectures; the privileged locus of the repetitions of trauma 'of which the patient himself was hitherto unaware' is related by Ferenczi to his guilt.
>
> (Sabourin, 1984, p. 14, translated)

Ferenczi had addressed this idea of the activation of the death drive by the other in "The adaptation of the family to the child" (Ferenczi, 1928) and "The unwelcome child and his death instinct" (Ferenczi, 1929).

The above considerations throw light on the debate concerning the Freud-Ferenczi dispute of the 1930s. The argument that Freud's anger with Ferenczi was due to the latter's having revived his early trauma theory is seen not to explain Freud's reaction. Again, it is found that the innovations introduced by Ferenczi in his text were accepted neither by Freud nor by the contemporary psychoanalytic community. Lastly, disagreement—not unrelated to the variations in Freud's theory at different times—is observed with regard to the unleashing of the death drive for, where Freud regards it as something structural and necessary that has always lain in wait, Ferenczi considers that the overflowing of the death drive results from the action of the other, an action that is traumatic because it exceeds the capacity of the infant's ego to register it within the framework of his own experience.

Trauma in the Clinical Diary

When Ferenczi says that there is a confusion of tongues, one must ask: what is it that is being confused? It is found that it is the child's language of tenderness that is being confused with adult erotic language. This confusion has a number of consequences, which are outlined as follows:

1   There is a state of affairs in which a trusted adult turns into an aggressor and destroys the child's security.
2   The child becomes paralyzed by intense fear.
3   The child identifies with the aggressor (at the same time introjecting the aggressor, who disappears as an external entity and becomes intra-psychic). The child wishes to gratify his attacker.
4   In this way, the child succeeds in maintaining the former situation and preserves the good image of the adult.
5   The child introjects the adult's sense of guilt.
6   Owing to his guilt, the child feels that his act deserves punishment.

The child is already divided, owing to his opposing feelings: he feels at one and the same time innocent and guilty. He is cut off from his own affective states and is pervaded by confusion. One part has recorded the experience, while another seeks to maintain the idea that nothing has happened.

The Adult's Response is a Contributory Factor to the Generation of Trauma

Ferenczi invokes three potentially traumatic situations: incestuous seductions, passionate punishments and the terrorism of suffering: *Erschütterung*. This German word is used repeatedly by Ferenczi throughout his late writings, for instance, in

Über Erschütterung ['On shock'] (Ferenczi, 1932b) and *Zur Revision der Traum-deutung* ['On the revision of the interpretation of dreams'] (Ferenczi, 1932c), both published in Volume 4 of his complete works in German, *Bausteine zur Psycho-analyse* (Ferenczi, 1940). The word is usually translated as 'shock,' or rendered directly as 'psychic shock,' and is derived, as Ferenczi explains, from "*schütten*, i.e. to become 'unfest, unsolid', to lose one's own form and to adopt easily and without resistance, an imposed form ('like a sack of flour')" (Ferenczi, 1932b, p. 254). According to the dictionary of Roudinesco and Plon (1998), in the entry on 'traumatic neuroses,' Freud uses the term *Erschütterung* in "Beyond the Pleasure Principle" (Freud, 1920) to denote the somatic character of trauma and *Schreck* [fright] for its psychic aspect.

Ferenczi refers to traumas or shocks occurring in early infancy (the first years of life). The level of the trauma depends on how early it takes place and on its impact:

> The stronger and more destructive the suffering – perhaps also the earlier in life it had to be endured, thus determining an orientation – the larger the circle of interests that must be drawn around the centre of the suffering in order to make it seem meaningful, or even naturally inevitable.
>
> (Dupont, 1985, pp. 31–32)

Later in the same text, Ferenczi writes:

> A helpless child is mistreated, for example, through hunger. What happens when the suffering increases and exceeds the small person's powers of comprehension? Colloquial usage describes what follows by the expression 'the child comes to be beside itself'. The symptoms of being beside oneself (seen from the outside) are: absence of reaction with regard to sensitivity, generalized muscle cramps, often followed by generalized paralysis ('being gone'). If I am to believe what my patients report about similar states, this 'being gone' is not necessarily a state of 'not-being', but rather one of 'not-being-here'.
>
> (Dupont, 1985, p. 32)

Trauma is thus connected with self-abandonment. This impacts how the event is remembered, as what has happened appears to be alien to the person himself: there is an externality about the suffering, as if it were being inflicted on someone else, and that is how the material enters consciousness, without any integration involving the patient. Ferenczi also suggests that schizophrenia is bound up with traumas sustained before the constitution of the personality.[2]

The fact that the child's adjustment to the environment is both untimely and imposed on him can also have traumatic effects (Dupont, 1985, p. 114). Not only indifference and aggression, but also excessive tenderness—that is, either an excess or a deficiency of these—has adverse effects on a child and may lead to a tendency to regress. For a child, Ferenczi holds, an excess of libidinal passion or its exaggerated expression can only be felt as aggression. The imposition of untimely forms of satisfaction on the child disturbs normal ego development, requiring the ego to confront tasks for which it is not equipped, being neither psychically nor emotionally mature enough to cope with them (Dupont, 1985, p. 189).

Ferenczi makes a further distinction between what he calls paternal and maternal hypnosis (the two concepts having been introduced in his paper "Introjection and transference" [Ferenczi, 1909]):

> Suggestibility, therefore, is actually the result of shock: paternal hypnosis equals fear of being killed, maternal hypnosis equals fear of being abandoned by the mother, that is, the threat that the libido will be withdrawn; the latter feels just as deadly as an aggressive threat to life. But the most frightful of frights is when the threat from the father is coupled with simultaneous desertion by the mother.
>
> (Dupont, 1985, p. 18)

These last two components, acting in unison, have the most catastrophic effects on the infant's psyche. Traumas will then impinge on a psyche that has fragmented. Ferenczi likens "when the anticathexis of the sensory organs is absent" (Dupont, 1985, p. 46). In this way, the resulting traumatic impression [*Eindruck*] can make its way without any resistance into the psyche, where it installs itself in the manner of a suggestion—that is, leaving the individual in a permanent state of hypnosis. The absence of countercathexis clearly influences the effect of the trauma. Ferenczi explains in his *Clinical Diary* (Dupont, 1985) what he means by being lost, which has to do with deception: a person's words convey the illusion that something is going to happen, but what actually occurs is something else or indeed the opposite of what was expected. So, the anticipated representation of the situation does not correspond to what happens in reality. It is this state of being lost or confused that is observed in the subject between surprise at the unexpected situation and subsequent adaptation. In children, however, the trauma occurs at times when no adult is available to repair the damage, but adaptation to the new situation is nevertheless called for:

> If the trauma strikes the soul or the body unprepared, that is, without countercathexis, then its effect is destructive for body and mind; that is, it disrupts through fragmentation [...]. In the psychic sphere, the intruding force, in the absence of a solid countercathexis, produces a kind of explosion, a destruction of psychic associations between the systems and psychic contents, which may reach down to the deepest elements of perception.
>
> (Dupont, 1985, pp. 69–70)

A number of aspects of Ferenczi's conception of splitting and fragmentation suggest that he sees splitting (in the sense of *Spaltung*) as a normal process, constitutive of the psyche and linked to loss, in which we encounter the first disappointments of love, related to weaning, sphincter control, punishment, education, etc. However, subsequent traumas and the absence of an appropriate environment and of adults who can accompany the child and help him to understand what is happening to him give rise to what Ferenczi calls the atomization of his personality. Ferenczi thus wonders: "But what is this being intolerable? Surely nothing else but continuing to live in a distorted inner (psychic) or outer reality" (Dupont, 1985, p. 192). Although the necessity of existing in fragmented, atomized form appears as a defence that allows the subject to go on living, it entails enormous and unbearable pain.

In Ferenczi's view, any psychic defence, whether neurotic or psychotic, leads in effect to the death of parts of the psyche:

> Whenever an emotional reaction is suppressed, interrupted, or repressed, something is actually destroyed in us. The annihilated part of the person falls into a state of decay and decomposes. Should the entire person be prevented from acting, then generalized decomposition ensues, that is to say, death. [...] Total disintegration (death) is just as impossible for it as coming back to life through the influx of vital energies.
>
> (Dupont, 1985, p. 88)

Trauma thus appears as a process of dissolution that tends towards death. That is why Ferenczi sees both neurotics and psychotics as being in the throes of a chronic death agony. The task of analysis, therefore, is fully to discover the nature of this death agony which patients carry with them, while also making them feel that in spite of everything, there is value in continuing to live—that it is worth existing.

For this reason, with regard to the treatment of these traumatized patients, Ferenczi emphasizes the importance of reaching the traumatic material. This can be explained as follows: at first, the trauma is accessible only by repetition, since it exists solely as 'something lived'; however, it is possible to relive it during analysis and turn it into an 'experience,' the outcome being the union of the fragmented parts of the personality.

The following quotation from Ferenczi will help us to understand the nature of trauma:

> What is trauma? 'Concussion', reaction to an 'unbearable' external or internal stimulus in an autoplastic manner (modifying the self) instead of an alloplastic manner (modifying the stimulus). A neoformation of the self is impossible without the previous destruction, either partial or total, or dissolution of the former self. A new ego cannot be formed directly from the previous ego, but from fragments, more or less elementary products of its disintegration. (Splitting, atomization.) The relative strength of the 'unbearable' excitation determines the degree and depth of the ego's disintegration.
>
> (Dupont, 1985, p. 181)

This passage further clarifies Ferenczi's previous statements that the factors which determine the depth of psychic fragmentation are the strength, insistence and intensity of the excitation. The earlier state to which the psychic fragments resulting from the subject's reaction to the trauma have given rise is completely changed. The fragmentation has to do with adaptation, in that it is precisely this which allows the subject to preserve the continuity of his existence.

Another question-and-answer passage points in the same direction:

> What is traumatic: an attack or its consequences? The adaptive potential 'response' of even very young children to sexual or other passionate attacks is much greater than one would imagine. Traumatic confusion arises mainly because the attack and the response to it are denied by the guilt-ridden adults, indeed, are treated as deserving punishment.
>
> (Dupont, 1985, p. 178)

Hence the child's attempt to adapt—that is, to make changes in his own psyche so as to confer meaning on, and respond to, the traumatic event—fails since it is not capable of maintaining a favourable state of affairs, because he is blamed both by the environment and by the people from whom he expects love and affection.

Conclusions

It is clear from the foregoing that Ferenczi's writings on trauma diverge appreciably from Freud's views while making an original contribution to psychoanalytic theory; at the same time, they provide a wealth of valuable indications for clinical practice. Throughout his final texts, Ferenczi argues that trauma is caused by the following state of affairs. A trusted adult turns into an aggressor, destroys the child's security and paralyzes him with fear. To preserve the former situation, the child identifies with the aggressor, introjecting him, causing him to disappear as an external threat, and converting him into an intra-psychic entity. In this way, he succeeds in maintaining the image of the adult prior to the aggression. The child introjects the adult's guilt and comes to feel that his act deserves punishment. The response of another adult, e.g. the mother, to this aggression, be it denial, approval, understanding, or otherwise, will be decisive in determining whether the outcome is traumatic. This response will be the basis on which the child will be able to start working through what has happened to him, or, conversely, on which he will disavow what he himself has lived through. The effect of trauma is fragmentation of the psyche; the difference between fragmentation and splitting is one of degree, and it depends on the insistency of the trauma whether a state of splitting leads on to fragmentation.

As a result of the psychic shock [*Erschütterung*] represented by the trauma, it remains unrecorded, even in the unconscious, and the traumatic element has to do with the impossibility of remembering. A stoppage of thought takes place, preventing the recording of any perception, and the person sinks into a state of passivity without putting up any kind of resistance. Analytic treatment must therefore make it possible for the patient to experience for the first time what he lived through traumatically.

Ferenczi and Freud quarrelled about trauma theory because, for Freud, Ferenczi was resuscitating a theory he had left behind in the development of psychoanalysis. Yet the dispute relates not only to the reality of trauma (as opposed to psychic reality), but also to the appearance and operation of the death drive, which for Freud is always present, whereas for Ferenczi it is triggered by a disorder of the environment or of another person. In Freud's case, certain passages in his works clearly indicate that he by no means ever completely discarded the trauma theory of his early writings.

Ferenczi's oeuvre occupies an enormously important place in the history of psychoanalysis and can throw light on the development of our discipline and present-day clinical practice. The last few years have witnessed a resurgence of interest in his writings among the psychoanalytic community, and the resulting advances have demonstrated the value of his insights to the full. His writings address fundamental psychoanalytic issues, relevant to both classical and contemporary psychoanalysis, with formulations that did not occur to others working at the same time. Furthermore, it was left to a whole new generation of analysts—even though most of them do not mention him—to bring analytic research to bear on these problems once again. As María Luisa Muñoz de la Cruz rightly pointed out in her opening address to the 1998 Congress on Ferenczi in Madrid:

> It seems to me that I speak for all of us in saying that what unites us at this wide-ranging symposium is not so much agreement or disagreement with Ferenczi's contributions, on the level of both theory and technique, as, above all, a communion with his 'psychoanalytic passion', his passion for psychoanalytic knowledge and research through, and in particular, on clinical work.
>
> (Muñoz de la Cruz, 1998, p. 9, translated)

What is important in Ferenczi's oeuvre, then, is not whether his solutions were right or wrong, but the issues raised in his writings, which are fundamental and remain unresolved to this day and stem from his clinical and analytic commitment.

Notes

1 Previously published in: Gutiérrez-Peláez, M. (2009). Trauma Theory in the 1931 and 1932 writings of Sandor Ferenczi. *International Journal of Psychoanalysis*, 90, 1217–1233.

2 "*Schizophrenia is a 'photochemical ' mimicry reaction*, instead of self-assertion (revenge, defense). (Dm.: schizophrenics were affected by trauma *before* they possessed a personality.)" (Dupont, 1985, p. 150).

Chapter 8

Ferenczi on the Suffering of the Child

> *[W]e, analysts (...) fail to notice that patients, although adults, have truly remained children who only want to play with things.*
>
> Ferenczi, *Clinical Diary* (1932d)

Introduction

Granoff (2004) poses a sharp question that is no trivial matter: Is it or is it not a child who suffers on the couch? And this question is not raised just anywhere, but at the very centre of a debate between two weighty figures: Sándor Ferenczi and Jacques Lacan. We find ourselves before a profound asymmetry, at a pivotal point where the positions cannot, by any means, be softened. They confront each other head-on from the outset—face to face and from opposing positions; polarities rather than dialectically reconcilable premises: "Is it truly a child on the couch?" (p. 111). Theoretical systems falter, and clinical approaches stumble.

Granoff completes his inquiry task, incisively aimed at tearing away veils to restore clarity (and in this sense, the question is no small matter):

> Is it a child who complains? Or is it an adult who complains? And this is where the issue becomes painful. If it is an adult – Freud or Lacan would say – then let him 'fix his head,' like a whining nuisance on the couch. But if it is a child, then everything is turned on its head, and even the secondary neurotic is at risk. A child's complaint is unsustainable! While an adult's complaint is merely unbearable.
>
> (p. 111)

How should we think about these two positions regarding the sufferer on the couch? How do such divergent perspectives arise? We set this question at the centre, but our lens focuses on Ferenczi, as his perspective seems darker, less accessible. It is well known that Ferenczi has been excluded from the history of psychoanalysis, a singular fact considering that his work is the most cited in the

DOI: 10.4324/9781003663324-8

theoretical production of his mentor, Freud (Jiménez Avello, 1998, p. 28). Both were latent and manifest readers of one another.

So, where do we anchor ourselves to account for this divergence? We establish a premise (temporary and fictional—in the Nietzschean sense—as a giver of meaning) to clarify the key points at play. This premise traverses the ever-open interstice of the *between*, like a tightrope stretched between two mountains—from pole to pole—between what the subject is and what it presents as its being: its silhouette seen from behind in the mirror, its camouflage, its recognition of itself through the voices of others, and what escapes this register.

We consider it as follows: for Lacan, the subject disguises itself as a child on the couch because it finds in this mimicry the only way to articulate its current problems. Therefore, the analyst does not operate as an archaeologist, tracing childhood experiences down to their origins in search of the golden insignias labelled *aetiology*. For Ferenczi, the matter is darker; he flips the coin, grounding himself at the other pole. He would consider—and here we speak on his behalf, hoping that in our words it is he who speaks through us, offering ourselves as a medium—that in certain moments of intense analytic regression, the subject *is* a child lying on the couch (and we emphasize the implications of this *is*). We might go further—always a possibility, especially with Ferenczi—and twist the statement to suggest that, for the Hungarian analyst, it is a child *disguised as an adult* who sits on the couch. The analytic process, much like removing the rusted plaques of an old, tarnished ornament, gradually reveals a subject (helpless and destitute: recall Freud's *Hilflösigkeit*) who has built severe layers for protection.

Ferenczi's Unique Clinical Perspective

We know that Ferenczi's patients are peculiar, that his clinical practice is highly distinctive, and even more singular are the psychic strata into which he delves. His clinical acuity serves as a compass guiding him to fundamental discoveries relevant to all psychic processes and clinical approaches. What does Ferenczi uncover in these patients? What unfolds for him as the zero point of the murky whirlpool of suffering? Here, we encounter the necessity of examining the particularities of his theory to understand what Ferenczi refers to when he speaks of trauma, *splitting*, *Erschütterung*, and the ruins of subjectivity.

Ferenczi's later contributions (as presented in Balint's compilation) reveal changes in both the form of his work and the interests that drive it. There is a unified essence in the content of the works from these years, making it coherent for Balint to present them as a single volume titled *Final Contributions to the Problems and Methods of Psychoanalysis*. The themes addressed in *Clinical Diary* (1932d) and *Reflections on Trauma* (1984d) showcase ideas about trauma and the psychic mechanisms involved, more so than fully developed theories. Ferenczi presents trauma as something that occurs in the encounter between an adult and a child, directly affecting the construction of the subject's narcissism.

In *Confusion of Tongues Between the Adults and the Child* (1932a), Ferenczi sets out to expand upon the topic of the external origin of trauma in relation to character and neurosis and to revisit the role of the traumatic factor, which has recurrently been read as building on earlier Freudian formulations. He differentiates between two currents of love at play: the tender and the erotic. The child, psychically, affectively, and biologically, is traversed by the former, while the latter is (in the best-case scenario) exclusive to adulthood. However, certain adults with psychopathological predispositions confuse the child's tender language with the sexual desires of a mature person and act on these perceptions without considering the consequences. What previously appeared as a game to the child, following the sexual act, transforms into something for which the child feels deserving of punishment. If the child manages to recover from such aggression, they are already divided, being both guilty and innocent, severing ties with their own feelings, perceptions, and senses, and falling into a state of confusion.

In this way, the child does not defend himself, but instead identifies with the aggressor and introjects that which appears threatening. Thus, the child's reaction signals the division of the personality. In other texts, Ferenczi (1929a) discusses how a child faces great fear when exposed prematurely to genital sensations, as their desires are aligned not with the violent passions of the adult but with play and tender affective expressions.

Trauma and the Fragmentation of the Psyche

The reaction triggered by trauma results in a rupture with reality, leading to the self-destruction of consciousness. This entails a cessation of thought and perception, paralyzing psychic functions and leaving no trace of those impressions, not even at the unconscious level. As such, there will be no way to recall what happened. The psychic apparatus does not retain any of these traumatic impressions. Genovés (in Jiménez Avello, 1998) suggests that this creates a "division of the personality," situating it pre-traumatically, denying that anything occurred. The attitude of the adult, pretending nothing has happened, enforces this forgetfulness, obstructs elaboration, and drives denial. This results in

> the self-destruction of consciousness and the cohesion of psychic formations into a singular entity, psychic paralysis with the consequence that no trace remains, not even in the unconscious. There is a dislocation of psychic functioning that leaves the event outside of mental registration.
>
> (p. 273)

Given the lack of mnemic impressions and therefore the impossibility of memory or the material coming into consciousness, it becomes evident that what is at play does not belong to the order of repression. In these Ferenczian theorizing, we clearly see the precursors to what Winnicott would later work on as "experiencing"—that is, giving the patient the chance to experience, within the analytic setting and with the help of the analyst, what they lived through but could not process as an experience at the time, due to their unprepared psychic state and the insufficiencies of their environment.

This *Erschütterung* (shock or psychic upheaval) that Ferenczi describes is marked by its peculiarity of always occurring without preparation for the sufferer. After initially being embedded with a sense of security, the child loses confidence in themselves and the world, either partially or entirely. The distress caused by this psychic upheaval becomes insurmountable, meaning no defence can address the surrounding world (*alloplastically*) to remove the source of suffering, nor can a representation be formed to process or elaborate it. Trauma immediately generates an overflow of anxiety, presenting as a sense of incapacity that prevents a favourable reaction to the situation—whether fleeing or eliminating the external danger. Consequently,

> Unpleasure increases and demands 'outlet'. Self-destruction as releasing some anxiety is preferred to silent toleration. Easiest to destroy in ourselves is the *cs* [consciousness] —the integration of mental images into a unit (physical unit is not such an easy prey to the impulses of self-destruction): Disorientation helps [...] directly, as a process of self-destruction (outlet).
>
> (Ferenczi, 1955b, p. 249)

Ferenczi states that a traumatic situation, which occurs unexpectedly, can produce an anaesthetic effect, understood as the total or partial cessation of psychic activity and the emergence of a state of passivity devoid of resistance. There is a halt to movement, perception, and thought. This loss of perception leads to the personality losing all forms of protection.

Confusion of Tongues and Fragmentation

Ferenczi (1932) explained that there is a confusion of tongues in the sense that the tender emotions of the child are interpreted as passionate by the adult, who reacts based on their own sexual predispositions, which are entirely different from what is accessible and possible for the child due to their infantile condition. The child, overwhelmed by fear, "automatically submits to the will of the aggressor, guesses their slightest desires, obeys completely, forgets themselves entirely, and identifies entirely with the aggressor" (p. 145).

This creates a clear rupture in the child's psyche, who becomes both the aggressor and the victim, experiencing guilt and pain that are irreconcilable. A psychic fragmentation has taken place in order to preserve the functioning of the psyche. Ferenczi explains this as follows:

> The offenses that the child commits, as if in play, are made real by the passionate punishments inflicted by curious, enraged adults, which, for an otherwise

innocent child, carry all the consequences of depression. A detailed examination
of the processes of analytic trance teaches us that there is no shock or fear without the announcement of a division of the personality.

(p. 147)

Such an experience of abuse will result in a premature psychic maturation of the
child.

In an entry of his *Clinical Diary* (1932d) titled "Fragmentation" (February
21st), Ferenczi discusses the advantages that fragmentation provides, particularly in terms of avoiding the displeasure that certain coherences might bring. For
example:

a child is the victim of overwhelming aggression, which results in 'giving up the
ghost' ['*Aufgeben des Geistes*'], with the firm conviction that this selfabandon-
ment (fainting) means death. However, it is precisely this complete relaxation
induced by self-abandonment that may create more favorable conditions for him
to endure the violence.

(p. 39)

The psychoanalytic treatment would then aim to help the patient discover that
this fragmented part of their personality is not dead. It becomes an arduous task
for the analysand to realize that life is worth living again, to recognize that they
are alive, and to understand that they sacrificed their integrity to save themselves.

Trauma and Childlike Expressions in Analysis

The traumatized patients who come to Ferenczi's office and reveal these issues
through their speech on the couch demonstrate a clear connection to their infantil-
ism. Ferenczi (1931a) explains: "the freer the process of association actually became, the more naive (one might say, the more childish) did the patient become in
his speech and his other modes of expressing himself" (p. 129). In the same essay,
"Child Analysis in Adult Analysis," Ferenczi notes similarities with descriptions
from child analysts and argues that there is not a significant difference, in terms
of suffering, between a child and an adult. For Ferenczi, it is clear that the fixation
point of his patients' illness is trauma experienced in early childhood. He asserts:

When you consider that, according to our experience hitherto and to the premises with which we start, most pathogenic shocks take place in childhood, you
will not be surprised that the patient, in the attempt to uncover the origin of his
illness, suddenly lapses into a childish or childlike attitude.

(p. 131)

It *is* a child, one must say, and here the affirmation returns: it is indeed a child
who lies on the couch; it is that psyche that associates, independent of its disguise.

In "Reflections on Trauma" (1984d), a series of notes published posthumously, Ferenczi specifies the effects of trauma on the psyche:

> Shock=annihilation of self-regard—of the ability to put up a resistance, and to act and think in defence of one's own self; perhaps even the organs which secure self-preservation give up their function or reduce it to a minimum. (The word *Erschütterung* is derived from *schütten*, i.e. to become 'unfest, unsolid', to lose one's own form and to adopt easily and without resistance, an imposed form— 'like a sack of flour').
>
> (p. 253)

The person abandons themselves in the face of the traumatic situation. There is a ruinous dismantling of subjectivity, a destruction of one's own person, and total surrender to the aggressor. This brings to mind the pseudo-humans that concentration camp inhabitants called *Muselmänner*, beings entirely alienated from themselves, avoided by others' gaze, existing in such distant lands that when they were killed, others hesitated to call it death (Agamben, 1999). In Ferenczi's traumatized patients, part of their personality becomes a *Muselmann*, while another part is like a camp resident who refuses to see, averts their gaze from what they do not wish to acknowledge, and yet feels it emerge, like a call of death, slowly, through every pore of their skin.

Psychic Fragmentation and the Role of the Analyst

It is possible to observe both a passive resistance to the attacks inflicted by the environment and a certain splitting of the self that presents, on one side, a suffering and shattered part, and on the other, a completely insensitive yet all-knowing part. Ferenczi writes: "It really seems as though, under the stress of imminent danger, a part of the self splits off to become a self-observing psychic agency that desires to help the self, and this possibly occurs in early – even the earliest – childhood" (1931a, p. 136). The patient returns to the place of these traumas in their sessions with such intensity that they quite literally inhabit and speak from that place to the extent that they are able. Following the trauma, "the creation of a new – displaced – situation of equilibrium" (p. 137) occurs. We have suggested naming these zones of equilibrium, which serve as links in the mind fragmented by trauma, "islands of ego integration." While these islands provide a certain integration and act as substitute supports for the psyche, they are fragile and prone to deterioration. Ideally, Ferenczi notes, they would dissolve during analysis, allowing the fragmented parts to settle on the solid ground provided by the analytic experience and the analyst's presence, enabling a beneficial primary experience for the first time.

Even with this exploration, we may still ask: How does a child reside within us, the so-called adults? This question inevitably leads to the question of the (a)temporality of the unconscious. It requires a reevaluation of common assumptions. To state that the unconscious is atemporal is inaccurate—or at least imprecise—since if there is no "before" and "after" in the unconscious, there is no way to account for the inscription of contents within it. It is more appropriate to use the distinction between *Historie* and *Geschichte*, terms employed by Heidegger and also by Freud in *Moses and Monotheism* (1964, p. 14). The unconscious has no *Historie* (chronological history); it contains no past events as such. Instead, what "has been" in the unconscious is always "being." This perpetual "being" allows the patient, in certain moments, to become a child on the couch or to populate their current world with faces from childhood. We know—and not only from reading Nietzsche—that when we lose the notion of time (a notion that, while mundane, is a significant claim), it is because, for a few moments (the paradox stands!), the present inhabits us.

Ferenczi's Bold Theoretical Horizons: Trauma and the Depths of the Psyche

Ferenczi takes us even further, beyond boundaries that already seem daring. This time, he aligns with another excluded figure: Jean-Baptiste Lamarck. Ferenczi invites us to experience, within the chaos of meanings in the sexual act, the history of catastrophes that traverse the living being. This history illustrates the concept of "always being": the emergence of continents, the threat of cellular desiccation, the separation of germ and soma and the consequent necessity of copulation, the ice age's correlation with the latency period, and all these events intertwined with the encounter with another body. In *Thalassa* (1924), Ferenczi depicts this encounter as a plunge into the infinite folds of life, folding and unfolding in an endless dance. The movement of the foreskin, the experience of being born, identification with the penis and semen, the bond with the other, and the "maternal peace" once felt in the womb—all these are connected to an ancient (and ever-present) point in our history.

This recalls the image of Govinda (from Hesse's *Siddhartha*, 1976), in one of those necessary topographies that seem too symbolic to be mere representations. Govinda observes Siddhartha's face, which ceases to be that of a man and becomes the face of his history: Govinda's history, Buddha's history, and that of all humans. A fish, death, the half-open mouth (both a yawn and a gateway to the soul), birth, old age, love, sacrifice, surrender, the becoming-animal, and the jaws of emotions—each pore a microcosm, an *Aleph*. Each human being is a continent of diverse lineages and ethnicities, of vegetal empires and cities built atop ancestral bodies. It is in this sense that, on the couch, everybody is the history of its body and the history of its history.

Chapter 9

Ferenczi's Concept of "Orpha"[1]

Introducing "Orpha"

There is a term that Ferenczi uses in his *Clinical Diary* (1932d)—and only there—a dark term that commentators have struggled to interpret, directly tied to memory processes regarding trauma. The term is "Orpha," which appears seven times throughout the *Diary* and twice as "orphic." Although Ferenczi provides few elements for its understanding, it may help clarify the nature of those traumatic memories that have never been conscious and must be experienced for the first time during psychoanalytic treatment. Stanton (1997) is probably the first commentator who has given a specific definition to this term, assigning it the status of a concept, highlighting its importance, and defining it based on Ferenczi's use in the *Clinical Diary*. Stanton defines it as follows:

> Orpha: A term derived from spiritualist terminology, denoting the creative destiny (following Orpheus, the god of poetry and imagination). This concept arises late in Ferenczi's career, primarily in response to his mutual analysis with Elisabeth Severn. For him, it represents unconscious, vital, and organizing instincts that nourish individuals and protect them from disintegration during moments of severe crisis.
>
> (p. 203)

Stanton's definition is intriguing for two main reasons: it positions "Orpha" as a concept related to disintegration and associates it with the analysis of Elisabeth Severn (a relationship between this patient and the notion of Orpha had been suggested earlier by Smith, 1998).

Elisabeth Severn and "Orpha"

Severn, who appears in the *Clinical Diary* as R.N., began analysis with Ferenczi in 1924. About her, he wrote to Groddeck, describing her as a "complex and troubling case" (letter dated July 27, 1928; cited by Stanton, 1997, p. 42). Later, in a letter dated December 21, 1930, he remarked:

> I dedicate four, sometimes five hours a day to my primary patient, 'the Queen' [Elisabeth Severn]. It is exhausting but rewarding. I think that soon—or at least,

DOI: 10.4324/9781003663324-9

not much longer—I will be able to say what it means to 'complete an analysis.' The other patients also 'enact' [*agieren*] vigorously and testify daily to why I have written about the necessity of reinstating the theory of seduction. In any case, psychoanalysis, as I am currently practicing it, draws more material from the patient than I previously anticipated.

(cited by Stanton, 1997, p. 46)

This patient, referred to by Ferenczi in various ways—including "my colleague" (Oxford Congress, 1929) and "Madame la Comtesse" (in a letter to Groddeck) (Stanton, 1997, p. 161)—was the principal subject of his technique known as "mutual analysis." Another mutual analysand was Clara Thompson, referred to in the *Clinical Diary* as Dm., who, as Stanton (1997) notes, "later helped found the Association for the Advancement of Psychoanalysis in New York and worked closely with Erich Fromm, Karen Horney, and Harry Stack Sullivan" (p. 195). He also mentions S. I. and B., all women, three of whom were American.

Thompson was a dancer, a Doctor of Philosophy, not unfamiliar with psychoanalysis, and authored several books: *Psychotherapy: Doctrine and Practice*, *The Psychology of Behavior*, and *The Discovery of the Self* (Stanton, 1997, pp. 161–168). Her work reflected a deep interest in spiritualist clairvoyance (Stanton, 1997, p. 165) and esoteric thought, leading to the likelihood that Ferenczi borrowed the term "Orpha" from the very words of his analysand.

In the *Diary* section titled "Who is crazy, we or the patients?" (May 1, 1932), Ferenczi states that there were "Immense resistance within myself, when, yielding to Orpha's proposal, I tried to allow myself to be analyzed by the patient;' that is, to surrender myself completely, to relax, and so to place myself in the patient's power" (1932d, p. 92). It is from this encounter with Elisabeth Severn and her "Orpha" that mutual analysis originates. It is through "Orpha" that Severn establishes her transferential bond with Ferenczi, believing she had found him telepathically (through a "teleplastic organ") because he was the only person in the world who could help her and repair the traumas of her childhood (see *"Counter-investment of Psychic Sensations That Become Intolerable," Clinical Diary*, June 12, 1932 entry).

Stanton aptly connects "Orpha" to spiritualist terminology and Orpheus, but it is necessary to take a step further to intertwine it with the role of memory and traumatic recollections.

Orphic Influences and the Role of Memory

In Greek philosophy, Pythagoras was the first to so emphatically take up the ancient Orphic traditions and incorporate them into his philosophical framework. With Pythagoras, the concept of the soul took a radically different turn:

The Pythagoreans, adopting the Orphic tradition, held the notion of the transmigration of souls. The idea is doubly significant; it definitively implies that the soul exists independently of the body. [...] The doctrine entails dualism, for the soul is a thing that dwells in the body, a captive in a prison or a prisoner in a dungeon. Hence, there is no organic relationship between the soul and the body. The naturalistic tendency toward viewing the soul as a product of the body's constitution was completely arrested by these influences. This dualism stems from a belief in an afterlife, and the mystical doctrine that the body is the tomb of the soul becomes, through Plato, the basis of all psychology that admits another life, whether obtained through transmigration, as in Orphism, or through resurrection, as in Christianity.

(Brett, 1964, p. 28)

This legacy of Orphic currents would strongly echo in Plato's later theory of reminiscence. Pythagorean thought endowed the soul with total independence, dissolving the connections previously conceived between the soul and body, intrinsically fused as a condition of existence. Plato revisited this Orphic notion to explore the role of memory:

A key to the correct solution is provided by memory. An experience often recalls another earlier one, and we are perfectly conscious that we are reliving the earlier experience through an act of the psyche. But in some cases, what is remembered has never been experienced in this life; remembrance, then, must be a reviving by the soul of experiences that belong to the soul itself. What is thus remembered is a truth independent of the present moment, a truth of an eternal nature.

(cited by Brett, 1964, p. 54)

Therefore, there would be a recalling of something that had never been experienced, which aligns with Ferenczi's observations regarding his traumatized patients. In Plato's philosophy, the soul is conceived as independent of the body.

Regarding his patient Elisabeth Severn, Ferenczi states in a section of the *Clinical Diary* (1932d) titled "Case of Progressive Schizophrenia" that the persistence of the traumas she had suffered (brutal sexual assaults) since early childhood led her to psychic fragmentation. During one session, there was a "sudden recollection of the events in the second year of life" (p. 8) associated with suicidal impulses, feelings of dying (agonies), and the loss of hope for any external help. "[B]ut as conscious thought is lost, or abandoned, the organizing life instincts ("Orpha") awaken, and in place of death allow insanity to intervene (The same "Orphic" powers appear to have been already present at the time of the first shock.)" (p. 8).

Ferenczi goes on to describe three distinct "fragments" that he identifies as composing his patient's psyche:

A being suffering purely psychically in his unconscious, the actual child, of whom the awakened ego knows absolutely nothing. This fragment is accessible only in deep sleep, or in a deep trance, following extreme exertion or exhaustion, that is, in a neurotic (hysterical) crisis situation. Only with great difficulty and by close observance of specific rules of conduct can the analyst make contact with this part: *the pure, repressed affect*.

(1932d, p. 8)

This reference to pure repressed affect connects to Freud's concept of *Spaltung* and primary repression as foundational to the psychic apparatus. However, as Pinheiro (1995) points out, there would be a distinction between a structuring trauma, which organizes the psychic apparatus, and a destructuring trauma, which leads to the fragmentation of the psyche.

Ferenczi describes another fragment of Severn's psyche as follows:

A singular being, for whom the preservation of life is of "coute que coute" significance. (Orpha.) This fragment plays the role of the guardian angel; it produces wish-fulfilling hallucinations, consolation fantasies; it anesthetizes the consciousness and sensitivity against sensations as they become unbearable. In the case of the second shock, this maternal part could not help in any other way than by squeezing the entire psychic life out of the inhumanly suffering body.

(1932, p. 9)

Lastly, he identifies a third fragment:

After the second shock, we therefore have to deal with a third, soulless part of the personality, that is to say, with a body progressively divested of its soul, whose disintegration is not perceived at all or is regarded as an event happening to another person, being watched from the outside.

(p. 9)

Returning to Plato's quote, intertwined with the Orphic currents as revived by Pythagoras, we observe a state of the psyche in which a part is alienated from itself, autonomous and ignorant of the suffering of the remaining parts. Additionally, there exists a condition of mnemonic material that has not been experienced; therefore, these traumatic experiences must be recovered during psychoanalytic treatment to be experienced for the first time.

Trauma and Its Effects

Trauma presents itself as a void—an absence that paradoxically produces effects across symptomatology, the subject's biography, and unconscious formations, such as in dreams. In Severn's case, her story is one of trauma: sexual and physical abuse from early childhood and throughout her youth. "The indefatigable Orpha, here, could not help itself any longer; it sought to encourage suicide. But as this was made impossible, the only form of existence left available was the complete atomization of psychic life" (1932, p. 10). This atomization resulted in:

> a kind of lifelessness. But the life of the body, compelled as it was to breathe and pulsate, called back Orpha, who in despair had herself become inclined toward death. She managed, however, as if by a miracle, to get this being back on its feet, shattered as it was to its very atoms, and thus procured a sort of artificial psyche for this body forcibly brought back to life. From now on the "individuum," superficially regarded, consists of the following parts: (a) uppermost, a capable, active human being with a precisely-perhaps a little too precisely-regulated mechanism; (b) behind this, a being that does not wish to have anything more to do with life; (c) behind this murdered ego, the ashes of earlier mental sufferings, which are rekindled every night by the fire of suffering; (d) this suffering itself as a separate mass of affect, without content and unconscious, the remains of the actual person.
>
> (1932, p. 10)[2]

Following Plato's framework, informed by Orphic traditions, there is a clear separation between psyche and body in Ferenczi's patient: a psyche that abandons all intentions of living and a body that manages to keep the person alive by creating an artificial psyche through its vital functions.

Conclusion

This analysis aimed to shed light on the obscure Ferenczian notion of "Orpha" by linking it to Platonic and Pythagorean traditions. "Orpha" relates to the effects of fragmentation (*splitting*), through which the patient defends against trauma. In such cases, a part of the person "dies" as a result of the traumatic event, while another, insensate, observes the events as if they were happening to someone else. The occultist influences of Ferenczi's renown patient, Elisabeth Severn, in whose context the references to "Orpha" appear, support the hypothesis regarding the origin of this concept.

Notes

1 A previous version of this chapter was published in: Gutiérrez-Peláez, M. (2008a). La noción ferencziana de "Orfa" [The Ferenczian notion of "Orpha"], *Revista Psicoanálisis*. XXX, 2/3, 285–290.
2 This will not be the only instance throughout his work where one feels they are reading Winnicott in Ferenczi. That "well-ordered mechanism" or "artificial double life" (Ferenczi, 1932d, p. 31), which conceals a fragmented state of the psyche, is undoubtedly a clear way of understanding what Winnicott conceptualizes as the "false self."

Chapter 10

Tongues, Trauma, and Transformation

Sándor Ferenczi occupies a unique position in the history of psychoanalysis. Though excluded and marginalized from the psychoanalytic movement, his writings and clinical understanding have gradually emerged as some of the most radical and generative contributions to the field. Over the course of this book, we have revisited Ferenczi's work through multiple lenses—psychoanalytic, historical, philosophical, and literary—in an effort to recover the richness of his insights and the enduring relevance of his thinking. In this final chapter, we seek to draw together the threads that have run throughout the previous ones, emphasizing the transformative potential that lies at the core of Ferenczi's vision of psychoanalysis, and illuminating the ways in which his thinking continues to reverberate through contemporary theory and practice.

One of the central ideas present in this volume is Ferenczi's preoccupation with language—not merely as a vehicle for communication, but as a psychic terrain through which trauma, desire, and survival are articulated. In Ferenczi, there is a conceptualization of the traumatic dimension of language, in an articulation that we can read retrospectively with Jacques Lacan's notion of the real and the presence in language of elements that exceed its symbolic function. Ferenczi's well-known formulation of the "Confusion of Tongues" goes beyond the dimension of sexual abuse and of a metaphorical statement about miscommunication between child and adult. It implies a fundamental ontological rupture. It is through language that trauma is both inflicted and, potentially, transformed, but not necessarily through interpretations or in its articulation with a determined symbolic system. That is the radical texture of Ferenczi's comprehension of trauma and language. His clinical work pushed him to look into ways to grasp within the psychoanalytic framework that which by itself is excluded from the symbolic properties of language. That is both the lucidity and the challenging nature of his clinical practice.

As we have seen in earlier chapters, the notion of analysis as a kind of translation underscores this point. Ferenczi's work invites us to think of translation not as a faithful reproduction of meaning, but as a transformative and often imperfect process of re-voicing. Translation itself, as made evident by Walter Benjamin and Jacques Derrida, deals with an impossibility: the inevitable *Spaltung* between languages and within each language. It is a structural schism and an unexcludable

DOI: 10.4324/9781003663324-10

presence of an absence. Though irrepresentable by its nature, an artistic representation of this crevice has been brilliantly staged in artist Doris Salcedo's work *Shibboleth* (Tate Modern in 2007): by creating a crack along the floor of the Tate Modern, spectators were inevitably interpellated by the abyss that exists between them.

The analyst does not decode what the patient says; they engage in an act of linguistic and affective mediation, attempting to give form to that which previously had no form, or to bring into representation that which had remained unspeakable. This conception of analysis as translation resonates with philosophical and literary conceptions of translation as reinvention—a way of generating something new out of fragments. It acknowledges that trauma cannot be directly expressed in language, but must be slowly and indirectly approached, interpreted, and reconfigured.

Closely linked to this conception of language is Ferenczi's radical reformulation of trauma. It is true that Ferenczi insisted on the real, external, and often violent origin of trauma and not only in its place as fantasies in the patient's psychic reality. For Ferenczi, trauma is often an actual event that overwhelms the psyche's capacity to process these experiences. His concept of *Erschütterung* captures this idea of psychic shock or upheaval, an encounter that disorganizes the self so profoundly that the subject must fragment in order to survive. This fragmentation is not metaphorical but structural: it implies a psychic rupture that cannot be resolved through standard interpretations or classic techniques.

What emerges from this rupture is not repression in the Freudian sense, but something more primal: a splitting that allows one part of the self to "play dead" while another part continues to function in a protective or dissociated manner. This splitting gives rise to the emergence of a substitute structure, artificial but necessary forms of psychic cohesion that maintain the minimum conditions for life, and which we have given the provisional name of "islands of ego integration." In his latest work, Ferenczi anticipates many developments in psychoanalysis and trauma theory, including concepts such as dissociation, the creation of false selves, and the establishment of protective identifications. His sensitivity to the subtleties of psychic fragmentation has influenced transformations in the psychoanalytic technique and has given rise to a broader understanding of subjectivity under conditions of extreme psychic suffering.

Ferenczi's study on psychic fragmentation, and with special emphasis on his work with his patient Elizabeth Severn, led him to the conceptualization of the enigmatic concept of Orpha. As explored in previous chapters, Orpha is the name he gives to the artificial, organizing force that sustains life in the wake of unbearable trauma. It is both a psychic invention and a survival mechanism, an internal caretaker that shields the subject from annihilation. Orpha does not heal the wound, nor does it integrate the trauma into a cohesive narrative. Rather, it keeps the organism alive in its presence, maintaining psychic life by creating a sort of parallel structure of coherence. This notion complicates the clinical aim of integration, suggesting that some psychic divisions, though possibly transitory, may be necessary and even life-sustaining.

Ferenczi's clinical innovations lay in his theoretical insights and in the ethical implications of his work. He imagined a different kind of analytic response—one grounded in tact, authenticity, and mutuality (in the technical use of this term). He called for an analyst who could bear witness to the patient's suffering without retreating into rigid technique or defensive neutrality. As I see it, Ferenczi sought, through his clinical innovations, to include within the analytic setup and treatment those unsymbolized, traumatic elements of the real, rather than leaving them outside the analyst's office, as sometimes seems to be the case with the loose understanding of concepts such as mutuality, relationality, and disclosure. This Ferenczian act was a bold departure that was not well received by his colleagues and that contributed to his epitome of *enfant terrible*. Ferenczi argued that the analyst's emotional availability and attunement were essential tools in the analytic process, and this contributed to his constant insistence on the importance of the rigorous analysis of the analyst.

In a sense, transformation undergirds a central theme in Ferenczi's legacy. This is not transformation in the sense of a complete resolution or idealized cure, but in the deeper sense of psychic transfiguration, which involves delving deep into the experience of the unconscious and creating something unique from within. What was once a source of unrepresentable suffering may, through the analytic process, become a site of gratification by creating a new link in the subject's relation to his own existence. This transformation is always precarious, partial, and for many of Ferenczi's patients, situated within the irreducible tension between trauma and survival. It is a transformation that implies a reconstruction and the slow reanimation of psychic life.

Ferenczi's work invites us to find today—with the challenges we face in contemporary clinical practice—a different way of listening, to conceptualize suffering in its deep implications and to take into account fully the ethical implications of our practice. His thought remains urgently alive. His unfinished and provocative writings will continue benefiting from further research. In returning to Ferenczi, we do not return to a work fixed in the history of psychoanalysis, but to a field of questions that remain vital to the psychoanalytic task: that of listening to those who consult us, from within their experiences of suffering, and of working through the elements they have identified as traumatic in their lives—an ongoing effort to weave their history from the most opaque resonances of language.

References

Agamben, G. (1999). *Remnants of Auschwitz: The Witness and the Archive*. New York, NY: Zone Books.

Agamben, G. (2005). *What is a device?* [Conference]. Paper presented at the University of La Plata, Argentina, October 12.

Auster, P. (1985). *The New York Trilogy*. London, UK: Faber and Faber.

Balint, M. (1969). *Clinical Diary* [Introduction]. Buenos Aires, Argentina: Conjetural.

Barzilai, S. (1997). History is not the past: Lacan's critique of Ferenczi. *Psychoanalytical Review*, *84*(4), 553–572.

Benet, J. (1990). *The Construction of the Tower of Babel*. Madrid, Spain: Siruela.

Berman, E. (1995). Confusion of tongues. *International Journal of Psychoanalysis*, *76*, 1045–1046.

Bion, W. R. (1962a). *Learning from Experience*. London, UK: Tavistock.

Bion, W. R. (1962b). The psycho-analytic study of thinking. *International Journal of Psychoanalysis*, *43*, 306–310.

Blum, H. P. (1994). The confusion of tongues and psychic trauma. *International Journal of Psychoanalysis*, *75*, 871–882.

Boorstin, D. J. (1994). *The Creators*. Barcelona, Spain: Crítica.

Borgogno, F. (2008). *Ferenczi and Winnicott: A partially missing link. Psicoanálisis*, *30*, 209–227.

Brett, G. S. (1964). *History of Psychology*. Buenos Aires, Argentina: Paidós.

Brook, J. A. (1992). Freud and splitting. *The International Review of Psychoanalysis*, *19*(3), 335–350.

Danto, E. A. (2005). *Freud's Free Clinics: Psychoanalysis and Social Justice, 1918–1938*. New York, NY: Columbia University Press.

Deleuze, G. (1967). *Nietzsche and Philosophy*. Barcelona, Spain: Anagrama. (Original title: Nietzsche et la philosophie)

Derrida, J. (1985). Des tours de Babel [The tower of Babel] (J. F. Graham, Trans.). *Differences: A Journal of Feminist Cultural Studies*, *3*(3), 165–207. (Original work published 1980)

Derrida, J. (1989). *Which One, Which: The Sources of Valéry*. In *Writing and Difference*. Barcelona, Spain: Anthropos.

Derrida, J. (1995). *Theology of Translation*. In *Language and Philosophical Institutions*. Spain: Paidós.

Derrida, J. (1997). *I – Psychoanalysis*. In *How Not to Speak and Other Texts*. Barcelona, Spain: Proyecto A.

Derrida, J. (1998a). *The Supplement of the Copula*. In *Margins of Philosophy*. Madrid, Spain: Cátedra. Translation from French to Spanish: Carmen González Martín, pp. 213–245. (Original work published 1989)

Derrida, J. (1998b). *The Ends of Man*. In *Margins of Philosophy*. Madrid, Spain: Cátedra.

Dupont, J. (Ed.). (1985). *The Clinical Diary of Sándor Ferenczi* (M. Balint & N. Zarday Jackson, Trans.). Cambridge, MA: Harvard University Press. (Original work published 1932 in French as Journal clinique (janvierjanvieroctobre 1932)

Dupont, J. (Ed.). (1988). *The Clinical Diary of Sándor Ferenczi* (M. Balint & N. Zarday Jackson, Trans.). Cambridge, MA: Harvard University Press.

Dupont, J. (1998). The concept of trauma according to Ferenczi and its effects on subsequent psychoanalytical research. *International Forum of Psychoanalysis, 7*, 235–240.

Eco, U. (1997). *What Do Those Who Don't Believe Believe In?* Bogotá, Colombia: Planeta. (Original title: In cosa credono quelli che non non?)

Erös, F. (2004). The Ferenczi cult: Its historical and political roots. *International Forum of Psychoanalysis, 13*, 121–128.

Evans, D. (1996). *An Introductory Dictionary of Lacanian Psychoanalysis.* London, UK: Routledge.

Eyre, D. P. (1975). A contribution to the understanding of the confusion of tongues. *International Journal of Psychoanalysis, 56*, 449–453.

Falzeder, E., & Brabant, E. (Eds.). (2000). *The Correspondence of Sigmund Freud and Sándor Ferenczi, Volume 3: 1920–1933.* Cambridge, MA: Belknap Press of Harvard University Press.

Ferenczi, S. (1909). *Introjection and Transference.* In E. Jones (Trans.), *First Contributions to Psycho-Analysis* (pp. 35–93). London, UK: Hogarth Press. (Original work published 1952)

Ferenczi, S. (1924). *Thalassa: A Theory of Genitality.* Buenos Aires, Argentina: Letra Viva.

Ferenczi, S. (1928). *The Adaptation of the Family to the Child.* In M. Balint (Ed.), *Final Contributions to the Problems and Methods of Psycho-Analysis* (pp. 61–76). London, UK: Hogarth Press.

Ferenczi, S. (1929a). *The Unwelcome Child and His Death Instinct.* In M. Balint (Ed.), *Final Contributions to the Problems and Methods of Psycho-Analysis* (pp. 102–107). London, UK: Hogarth Press.

Ferenczi, S. (1929b). *Relaxation and Neocatharsis.* In *Obras Completas* (Vol. IV). Madrid, Spain: Espasa-Calpe.

Ferenczi, S. (1930–1932). *Notes and Fragments.* In M. Balint (Ed.), *Final Contributions to the Problems and Methods of Psycho-Analysis* (pp. 216–279). London, UK: Hogarth Press.

Ferenczi, S. (1931a). *Child-Analysis in the Analysis of Adults.* In M. Balint (Ed.), *Final Contributions to the Problems and Methods of Psycho-Analysis* (pp. 126–142). London, UK: Hogarth Press.

Ferenczi, S. (1931b). *Trauma and Anxiety.* In M. Balint (Ed.), *Final Contributions to the Problems and Methods of Psycho-Analysis* (pp. 249–250). London, UK: Hogarth Press.

Ferenczi, S. (1932a). *Confusion of Tongues between Adults and the Child.* In M. Balint (Ed.), *Final Contributions to the Problems and Methods of Psycho-Analysis* (pp. 156–167). London, UK: Hogarth Press.

Ferenczi, S. (1932b). *On Shock [Über Erschütterung].* In M. Balint (Ed.), *Final Contributions to the Problems and Methods of Psycho-Analysis* (pp. 253–254). London, UK: Hogarth Press.

Ferenczi, S. (1932c). *On the Revision of the Interpretation of Dreams [Zur Revision der Traumdeutung].* In M. Balint (Ed.), *Final Contributions to the Problems and Methods of Psycho-Analysis* (p. 240). London, UK: Hogarth Press.

Ferenczi, S. (1932d). *Clinical Diary.* Buenos Aires, Argentina: Conjetural.

Ferenczi, S. (1933a). Confusion of tongues between adults and the child [Sprachverwirrung zwischen den Erwachsenen und dem Kind]. *Internationale Zeitschrift Für Psychoanalyse, 19*, 5–15.

Ferenczi, S. (1933b). Confusion of tongues between the adults and the child: The language of tenderness and of passion. *International Journal of Psycho-Analysis, 30*, 225–230.

Ferenczi, S. (1940). *Bausteine zur Psychoanalyse* (Vols. 1–3). Bern, Switzerland: Huber.

Ferenczi, S. (1955a). *The Unwelcome Child and His Death Instinct*. In M. Balint (Ed.), *Final Contributions to the Problems and Methods of Psycho-Analysis* (pp. 102–107). London, UK: Karnac Books. (Original work published 1929)

Ferenczi, S. (1955b). *Notes and Fragments*. In M. Balint (Ed.), *Final Contributions to the Problems and Methods of Psycho-Analysis* (pp. 216–279). London, UK: Karnac Books. (Original work published 1939)

Ferenczi, S. (1955c). *Trauma and Anxiety*. In M. Balint (Ed.), *Final Contributions to the Problems and Methods of Psycho-Analysis* (pp. 249–250). London, UK: Karnac Books. (Original work published 1931)

Ferenczi, S. (1955d). *Confusion of Tongues Between Adults and the Child*. In M. Balint (Ed.), *Final Contributions to the Problems and Methods of Psycho-Analysis* (pp. 156–167). London, UK: Karnac Books. (Original work published 1933)

Ferenczi, S. (1955e). *Final Contributions to the Problems and Methods of Psycho-Analysis* (M. Balint Ed.). London, UK: Karnac Books.

Ferenczi, S. (1968). *Thalassa: A Theory of Genitality*. New York, NY: Norton. (Original work published 1924)

Ferenczi, S. (1981). *Science That Sleeps, Science That Awakens*. In M. Balint (Ed.) & F. J. Aguirre (Trans.), *Complete Works* (Vol. III). Madrid, Spain: Espasa-Calpe. (Original work published 1924)

Ferenczi, S. (1984a). *Confusion of Tongues Between Adults and the Child: The Language of Tenderness and Passion*. In M. Balint (Ed.) & F. J. Aguirre (Trans.), *Complete Works* (Vol. IV, pp. 123–135). Madrid, Spain: Espasa-Calpe. (Original work published 1932a)

Ferenczi, S. (1984b). *Child Analysis in the Analysis of Adults*. In M. Balint (Ed.) & F. J. Aguirre (Trans.), *Complete Works* (Vol. IV). Madrid, Spain: Espasa-Calpe. (Original work published 1931)

Ferenczi, S. (1984c). *The Problem of the End of Analysis*. In M. Balint (Ed.) & F. J. Aguirre (Trans.), *Complete Works* (Vol. IV). Madrid, Spain: Espasa-Calpe. (Original work published 1928)

Ferenczi, S. (1984d). *Reflections on Trauma*. In M. Balint (Ed.) & F. J. Aguirre González (Trans.), *Complete Works* (Vol. IV, pp. 153–163). Buenos Aires, Argentina: Amorrortu. (Original work published 1934)

Ferenczi, S. (1984e). La adaptación de la familia al niño [The adaptation of the family to the child]. In J. Jiménez Lozano, J. L. Etcheverry, & J. J. del Cura (Eds.), *Obras completas, psicoanálisis* (Vol. III, Chap. I, pp. 313–324). Madrid, Spain: Espasa-Calpe.

Ferenczi, S. (1985a/1932c). *Clinical Diary*. Buenos Aires, Argentina: Conjetural.

Ferenczi, S. (1985b). *Foundations of Psychoanalysis, Vol. IV: Memorial Articles, Critiques, Reviews, and Fragments*. Leipzig, Germany: Ullstein Materialien. (Originally published 1940 as Bausteine zurzurPsychoanalyse)

Ferenczi, S. (1990–2019). *Œuvres complètes* (Vols. 1–4). Paris: Payot.

Ferenczi, S. (1997/1932d). *Clinical Diary: Without Sympathy, There Is No Healing*. Buenos Aires, Argentina: Amorrortu.

Ferenczi, S. (2002a). *The Dream of the Clever Baby*. In J. Rickman (Ed.) & O. Edmonds (Trans.), *Further Contributions to the Theory and Technique of Psychoanalysis* (pp. 349–350). London, UK: Karnac Books. (Original work published 1923)

Ferenczi, S. (2002b). *On the Symbolism of the Head of Medusa*. In J. Rickman (Ed.) & O. Edmonds (Trans.), *Further Contributions to the Theory and Technique of Psychoanalysis* (p. 360). London, UK: Karnac Books. (Original work published 1923)

Ferenczi, S. (2002c). *Notes and Fragments*. In J. Dupont (Ed.) & E. & M. Bálint (Trans.), *The Complete Psychoanalytic Works of Sándor Ferenczi* (Vol. 3, pp. 363–443). London: Karnac.

Ferenczi, S. (2003). *Confusion of tongues between the adult and the child. The International Journal of Psychoanalysis, 30*, 225–230. (Originally published 1932b/1949)

Ferenczi, S. (2012). *Confusion of Tongues Between the Adult and the Child.* In M. Gutiérrez-Peláez (Ed.) & M. Gutiérrez-Peláez & M. Rojas (Trans.), *Confusion of Tongues: A Return to Sándor Ferenczi* (pp. 247–260). Mar del Plata, Argentina: EUDEM. (Original work published 1932e)

Ferenczi, S., & Groddeck, G. (2002). *The Sándor Ferenczi–Georg Groddeck Correspondence 1921–1933* (C. Fortune, Ed.). London, UK: Open Gate Press.

Ferenczi, S., & Rank, O. (1924). *The Development of Psychoanalysis* (C. Newton, Trans.). Madison, CT: International Universities Press. (Original work published 1986)

Fergusson, A. (2015). *Imaginary Letters to Freud and Other Essays.* Bogotá, Colombia: Editorial Universidad del Rosario.

Fergusson, A., & Gutiérrez-Peláez, M. (2022). *Sándor Ferenczi: A Contemporary Introduction.* Routledge.

Frankel, J. (2002). Exploring Ferenczi's concept of identification with the aggressor: Its role in trauma, everyday life, and the therapeutic relationship. *Psychoanalytic Dialogues, 12,* 101–139.

Frankel, J. (2004). Identification with the aggressor and the "normal traumas": Clinical implications. *International Forum of Psychoanalysis, 13,* 78–83.

Freud, S. (1896). Further remarks on the neuro-psychoses of defence. *The Standard Edition of the Complete Psychological Works of Sigmund Freud, 3,* 157–185.

Freud, S. (1905). Three essays on the theory of sexuality. *SE, 7,* 123–246.

Freud, S. (1914). On the history of the psycho-analytic movement. *SE, 14,* 1–66.

Freud, S. (1918). From the history of an infantile neurosis ("Wolf Man"). *SE, 17,* 1–124.

Freud, S. (1920). Beyond the pleasure principle. *SE, 18,* 1–64.

Freud, S. (1923). The ego and the id. *SE, 19,* 1–66.

Freud, S. (1926). *Inhibición, síntoma y angustia [Inhibition, symptom and anxiety].* In J. L. Etcheverry (Ed. & Trans.), *Obras completas* (Vol. XX, pp. 75–176). Buenos Aires, Argentina: Amorrortu.

Freud, S. (1938a). *Esquema del psicoanálisis [An outline of psychoanalysis].* In J. L. Etcheverry (Ed. & Trans.), *Obras completas* (Vol. XXIII, pp. 141–207). Buenos Aires, Argentina: Amorrortu.

Freud, S. (1938b). *Moisés y la religión monoteísta [Moses and monotheism].* In J. L. Etcheverry (Ed. & Trans.), *Obras completas* (Vol. XXIII, pp. 1–138). Buenos Aires, Argentina: Amorrortu.

Freud, S. (1955). *Medusa's Head.* In J. Strachey (Ed. & Trans.), *The Standard Edition* (Vol. 18, pp. 273–274). London, UK: Hogarth Press. (Original work published 1940)

Freud, S. (1957). *Instincts and their Vicissitudes.* In J. Strachey (Ed. & Trans.), *The Standard Edition of the Complete Psychological Works of Sigmund Freud* (Vol. 14, pp. 109–140). London: Hogarth Press. (Original work published 1915)

Freud, S. (1964). Moses and Monotheism. In J. Strachey (Ed.) & J. Strachey & K. Jones (Trans.), *The Standard Edition of the Complete Psychological Works of Sigmund Freud* (Vol. 23, pp. 1–137). London: Hogarth Press. (Original work published 1939)

Freud, S. (1976a). *Contribution to the History of the Psychoanalytic Movement.* In J. Strachey (Ed.) & J. L. Etcheverry & L. Wolfson (Trans.), *Complete Works* (Vol. XIV, pp. 1–64). Buenos Aires, Argentina: Amorrortu. (Original work published 1914)

Freud, S. (1976b). *Doctor Sándor Ferenczi (On His 50th Birthday).* In J. Strachey (Ed.) & J. L. Etcheverry & L. Wolfson (Trans.), *Complete Works* (Vol. XIX, pp. 287–289). Buenos Aires, Argentina: Amorrortu. (Original work published 1923)

Freud, S. (1976c). *Sándor Ferenczi.* In J. Strachey (Ed.) & J. L. Etcheverry & L. Wolfson (Trans.), *Complete Works* (Vol. XXII, pp. 226–228). Buenos Aires, Argentina: Amorrortu. (Original work published 1933)

Freud, S. (2002). *Letter from Sigmund Freud to Karl Abraham, August 27, 1918.* In E. Falzeder (Ed.), & C. Schwarzacher (Trans.), *The Complete Correspondence of Sigmund Freud and Karl Abraham, 1907–1925* (pp. 381–382). New York, NY: Basic Books.

Freud, S. (2003a). *A Seventeenth-Century Demonological Neurosis.* In J. Strachey (Ed.) & J. L. Etcheverry (Trans.), *Complete Works* (Vol. 19, pp. 67–106). Buenos Aires, Argentina: Amorrortu.

Freud, S. (2003b). *Correspondence With Fliess: Letter 69.* In J. Strachey (Ed.) & J. L. Etcheverry (Trans.), *Complete Works* (Vol. 1, pp. 301–302). Buenos Aires, Argentina: Amorrortu.

Freud, S. (2003c). *Drives and Their Vicissitudes.* In J. Strachey (Ed.) & J. L. Etcheverry (Trans.), *Complete Works* (Vol. 14, pp. 105–134). Buenos Aires, Argentina: Amorrortu. (Original work published 1915)

Freud, S. (2003d). *Further Remarks on the Neuro-Psychoses of Defence.* In J. Strachey (Ed.) & J. L. Etcheverry (Trans.), *Complete Works* (Vol. 3, pp. 157–184). Buenos Aires, Argentina: Amorrortu.

Freud, S. (2003e). *My Views on the Role of Sexuality in the Aetiology of the Neuroses.* In J. Strachey (Ed.) & J. L. Etcheverry (Trans.), *Complete Works* (Vol. 7, pp. 259–272). Buenos Aires, Argentina: Amorrortu.

Freud, S. (2003f). Negation. In J. Strachey (Ed.) & J. L. Etcheverry (Trans.), *Complete Works* (Vol. 19, pp. 249–258). Buenos Aires, Argentina: Amorrortu.

Fulcanelli (1922). *The Mystery of the Cathedrals.* Spain: Biblioteca Fundamental Año Cero. *(Original title: Le MystèreMystèreCathédrales)*

Gay, P. (1989). *Freud: A Life for Our Time.* Barcelona, Spain: Paidós.

Granoff, W. (1988). *Freud as Writer: Translate or Standardize?* In P. Garrido & G. Leff (Eds.), *Lacan, Ferenczi, and Freud* (pp. 147–168). Buenos Aires, Argentina: École Lacanienne de Psychanalyse.

Granoff, W. (2004). *Lacan, Ferenczi, and Freud.* Buenos Aires, Argentina: École Lacanienne de Psychanalyse.

Graves, R. (1985). *The Greek Myths*, Vols. I & II. Madrid, Spain: Alianza.

Gutiérrez-Peláez, M. (2007). Translation and confusion of tongues [Sobre la traducción y la confusión de lenguas]. *Revista Universitaria de Psicoanálisis* (RUP), 7, 51–69.

Gutiérrez-Peláez, M. (2008a). The Ferenczian Notion of "Orpha." *Revista de Psicoanálisis*, 30(2/3), 285–290.

Gutiérrez-Peláez, M. (2008b). War neuroses in the history of the psychoanalytic movement. *Revista Universitaria de Psicoanálisis*, 8, 203–216.

Gutiérrez-Peláez, M. (2009). Trauma theory in the 1931 and 1932 writings of sándor ferenczi. *International Journal of Psychoanalysis*, 9(6), 1217–1233.

Gutiérrez-Peláez, M. (2010). Differences between the concepts of splitting in ferenczi and *spaltung* in freud. *Universitas Psychologica*, 9(2), 469–483.

Gutiérrez-Peláez, M. (2012). *Confusion of Tongues: A Return to Sándor Ferenczi.* Mar del Plata, Argentina: EUDEM.

Gutiérrez-Peláez, M. (2021). Not knowing and not wanting to know: Reflections regarding psychosocial and psychotherapeutic interventions in armed conflict scenarios. *Psychoanalytic Psychology*, 38(4), 348–351. https://doi.org/10.1037/pap0000341

Harris, A., & Aron, L. (1997). Ferenczi's semiotic theory: Previews of postmodernism. *Psychoanalytic Inquiry*, 17, 522–534.

Heidegger, M. (1955). *What Is That—Philosophy?* Buenos Aires, Argentina: Sur. *(Original title: Was ist das—die Philosophie?) das—die Philosophie?)*

Heller-Roazen, D. (2008). *Echolalias: On the Forgetting of Language.* New York, NY: Zone Books.

Hesse, H. (1976). *Siddhartha.* Spain: Bruguera.

Hidas, G. (1993, July 21). *History of Hungarian Psychoanalysis*. Unpublished presentation at the Fourth International Conference of the Sándor Ferenczi Society, Budapest, Hungary.

Hinshelwood, R. D. (1989). *Dictionary of Kleinian Thought*. Buenos Aires, Argentina: Amorrortu.

Hunyady, O. (2012). Herr professor and his "Grand vizir": The Freud/Ferenczi relationship in its social context. *Contemporary Psychoanalysis, 48*(2), 166–182.

Jacobson, J. G. (1994). Signal affects and our psychoanalytic confusion of tongues. *Journal of the American Psychoanalytic Association, 42*, 15–42.

Jakobson, R. (1968). *Child Language, Aphasia, and Phonological Universals*. The Hague, The Netherlands: Mouton.

Jiménez Avello, J. (with Genovés, A.). (1998). *Reading Ferenczi*. Madrid, Spain: Biblioteca Nueva.

Johnson, P. (2004). *A History of the Jews*. Barcelona, Spain: Vergara.

Jones, E. (1953). *The Life and Work of Sigmund Freud*. New York, NY: Basic Books.

Juliet, C. (2006). *Encounters With Samuel Beckett*. Madrid, Spain: Siruela.

Krull, M. (1979). *Freud and His Father: The Origin of Psychoanalysis and Freud's Unresolved Bond With His Father*. Munich, Germany: C. H. Beck. *(Original title: Freud und sein Vater, die EntstehungEntstehungPsychoanalyse und Freuds ungelösteungelöste Vaterbindung)*

Lacan, J. (1967). *Brief Discourse of Jacques Lacan to Psychiatrists* [Unpublished manuscript].

Lacan, J. (1974–1975). *The Seminar, Book XXII: RSI*. Buenos Aires, Argentina: Ornicar. *(Original seminar delivered 1974–1975)*

Lacan, J. (1975). *The Seminar of Jacques Lacan: Book I. Freud's Papers on Technique, 1953–1954* (J.-A. Miller, Ed.; J. Forrester, Trans.). New York, NY: Norton.

Lacan, J. (1997). *The Seminar, Book XX: Encore [Aún]* (J.-A. Miller, Ed.). Buenos Aires, Argentina: Paidós. (Original seminar given 1972–1973)

Lacan, J. (1998). *The Four Fundamental Concepts of Psychoanalysis* (J.-A. Miller, Ed.; A. Sheridan, Trans.). London, UK: Norton. (Original seminar given 1964)

Lacan, J. (2002). *The Direction of the Treatment and the Principles of Its Power*. In B. Fink (Ed.), *Écrits: The First Complete Edition in English* (pp. 489–542). New York, NY: Norton. (Original work published 1958)

Lacan, J. (2006a). *The Function and Field of Speech and Language in Psychoanalysis (1953)*. In B. Fink (Trans.), *Écrits: The First Complete Edition in English* (pp. 197–268). New York, NY: Norton.

Lacan, J. (2006b). *Variants of the Standard Treatment*. In B. Fink (Trans.), *Écrits: The first Complete Edition in English* (pp. 267–308). New York, NY: W. W. Norton & Company. (Original work published 1955)

Lacan, J. (2007). *The Seminar, Book XXIII: The Sinthome*. Buenos Aires, Argentina: Paidós. (Original seminar given 1975–1976)

Lacan, J. (2009). *The Seminar, Book XVIII: Of a Discourse That Would Not Be of the Semblant*. Buenos Aires, Argentina: Paidós. (Original seminar given 1971)

Laplanche, J., & Pontalis, J.-B. (1997). *Dictionary of Psychoanalysis*. Buenos Aires, Argentina: Paidós.

Lugrin, Y. (2017). *Ferenczi sur le divan de Freud: une analyse* finie? Paris : Campagne Première.

Márai, S. (1933, June 14). *The Living and the Dead. Brassói Lapok*, pp. 11–12. (Original title: Élők és holtak)

Márai, S. (1999a). *The living and the dead. Thalassa, 1*, 151–153.

Márai, S. (2000). *The Living and the Dead: In Memoriam Sándor Ferenczi*. In J. Mészáros (Ed.), (pp. 47–50). Budapest, Hungary: Jószöveg. *(*Original title: Élők és holtak. In memoriam Ferenczi Sándor)

Márai, S. (2008). *Diaries 1984–1989*. Barcelona, Spain: Salamandra.

Masson, J. M. (1984). *The Assault on Truth: Freud's Suppression of the Seduction Theory*. London, UK: Faber & Faber.

Matamoros, B. (1998). *America in the Tower of Babel*. São Paulo, Brazil: University of São Paulo.

Mészáros, J. (1999). *Toward Psychoanalysis: Ferenczi Sándor's Early Writings, 1897–1908*. Budapest, Hungary: Osiris. (Original title: A pszichoanalízispszichoanalízisfelé. Ferenczi Sándor: IfjukoriIfjukoriírások 1897–1908)

Mészáros, J. (2000). *In Memoriam Sándor Ferenczi*. Budapest, Hungría: Jószöveg Publishing House.

Mészáros, J. (2010). Sándor Ferenczi and the Budapest school of psychoanalysis. *Psychoanalytical Perspectives, 7*, 69–89.

Mészáros, J. (2014). *Ferenczi and Beyond: Exile of the Budapest School and Solidarity in the Psychoanalytic Movement During the Nazi Years*. London, UK: Karnac Books.

Mészáros, J., Harmatta, J., & Bókay, A. (Eds.). (2022). *Ferenczi a Pszichoanalízis Felé*: Preanalitikus Írások, *1897–1908* [Ferenczi Toward Psychoanalysis: Preanalytic Writings, *1897–1908*]. Oriole és Társai.

Miller, G. (Director). (2011). *Meeting With Lacan* [Motion picture]. Paris, France: Penelope 2 Cafés L'Addition. (Original title: Rendez-vous chez Lacan)

Miller, J.-A. (2008). *Lecture at the Coliseo Theater*. In G. Brodsky (Eds.), *Portenian Lectures*, (Vol. III, pp. 257–276). Buenos Aires, Argentina: Paidós. (Original title: Conferencia en el Teatro Coliseo)

Milton, J. (1667). *Paradise Lost*. Mexico City, Mexico: Diana.

Modell, A. H. (1991). A confusion of tongues or whose reality is it? *The Psychoanalytic Quarterly, 60*, 227–244.

Muñoz de la Cruz, M. L. (1998). The clinical diary: Interdependence between clinical work and psychoanalytic technique. Points of agreement and differences. *Revista de Psicoanálisis de la Asociación Psicoanalítica de Madrid, 28*, 9–14.

Nietzsche, F. (1980). *The Wanderer and His Shadow*. Madrid, Spain: Alianza.

Nietzsche, F. (2001). *The Gay Science*. Spain: Akal.

Nietzsche, F. (2003). *Thus Spoke Zarathustra*. Madrid, Spain: Alianza.

Parrot, A. (1961/1962). *La Torre de Babel [The Tower of Babel] (J. R. Bargas, Trans.)*. Barcelona, Spain: Ediciones Garriga. (Cuadernos de Arqueología Bíblica, 2)

Pinheiro, T. (1995). *From the Cry to the Word*. Rio de Janeiro, Brazil: UFRJ.

Press, J. (2006). Constructing the truth: From "Confusion of tongues" to "Constructions in analysis". *International Journal of Psychoanalysis, 87*(2), 519–537.

Rachman, A. W. (1989). Confusion of tongues: The Ferenczian metaphor for childhood seduction and emotional trauma. *Journal of the American Academy of Psychoanalysis, 17*, 181–205.

Rachman, A. W. (1997). The suppression and censorship of Ferenczi's "Confusion of tongues" paper. *Psychoanalytic Inquiry, 17*, 459–485.

Roudinesco, E., & Plon, M. (1997). *Dictionary of Psychoanalysis*. Paris, France: Fayard.

Roudinesco, E., & Plon, M. (1998). *Dictionary of Psychoanalysis*. Buenos Aires, Argentina: Paidós.

Sabourin, P. (1984). *Foreword: Secret Vizier and Scapegoat*. In S. Ferenczi (Ed.), *Clinical Diary* (pp. 11–20). Buenos Aires, Argentina: Amorrortu. (Original title: Prefacio. Visir secreto y cabeza de y cabeza de)

Sabsay Foks, G. (2011). Ferenczi in Argentina. In P. Boschan (Ed.), *Sándor Ferenczi and 21st Century Psychoanalysis* (pp. 425–431). Buenos Aires, Argentina: Letra Viva.

Schur, M. (1972). *Freud: Living and Dying*. New York, NY: International Universities Press.

Sgalambro, M. (1996). *Good Cannot Be Founded on a Homicidal God*. In U. Eco & C. M. Martín (Eds.), *What Do Those Who Don't Believe Believe In?* Bogotá, Colombia: Planeta. (Original title: El bien no puede fundarse en un Dios homicida)

Shepherdson, C. (2008). *Lacan and the Limits of Language*. Bronx, NY: Fordham University Press.

Smith, N. A. (1998). Orpha reviving. *International Forum of Psychoanalysis*, 7, 241–246.

Stanton, M. (1997). Sándor Ferenczi: Reconsidering Active Technique. *Bio-Psique*, Chile.

Sulloway, F. (1979). *Freud: Biologist of the Mind*. New York, NY: Basic Books.

Sylwan, B. (1984). An untoward event: *Ou la guerre du trauma de Breuer à Freud de Jones à Ferenczi. Cahiers Confront*, 2, 101–115.

Toboul, B. (2005). *Condensation, metaphor, and the real: Or the structure revisited. Figures de la psychanalyse*, 11, 33–61. (Original title: La condensation, la métaphore et le réel, ou la structure revisitée)

Weibel, P. (2005). *Biographical Sketches of the Psychoanalytic Movement*. In P. Weibel (Ed.), *Beyond Art, a Third Culture: A Comparative Study in Cultures, Art, and Science in 20th Century Austria and Hungary* (pp. 511–514). London, UK: Springer.

Willson, P. (2004). *The Southern Constellation: Translators and Translations in 20th-Century Argentine Literature*. Buenos Aires, Argentina: Siglo XXI. (Original title: La constelación del sur: traductores y traducciones en la literatura argentina del siglo XX)

Winnicott, D. W. (1954/1979). *Metapsychological and Clinical Aspects of Regression Within the Psychoanalytic Frame*. In C. B. Winnicott, R. Shepherd, & M. Davis (Eds.), *Escritos de pediatría y psicoanálisis [Writings on Pediatrics and Psychoanalysis]* (pp. 281–294). Barcelona, Spain: Laia.

Winnicott, D. W. (1955–1956/1979). *Clinical Varieties of Transference*. In C. B. Winnicott, R. Shepherd, & M. Davis (Eds.), *Escritos de pediatría y psicoanálisis [Writings on Pediatrics and Psychoanalysis]* (pp. 451–470). Barcelona, Spain: Laia.

Winnicott, D. W. (1958). Ernest Jones. *International Journal of Psychoanalysis*, 29, 127.

Winnicott, D. W. (1959/1993). *Classification: Is There a Psychoanalytic Contribution to Psychiatric Classification?* In C. B. Winnicott, R. Shepherd, & M. Davis (Eds.), *Los procesos de maduración y el ambiente facilitador [The Maturational Processes and the Facilitating Environment]* (pp. 120–136). Barcelona, Spain: Laia.

Winnicott, D. W. (1963/1989). *Fear of Breakdown*. In C. Winnicott, R. Shepherd, & M. Davis (Eds.), *Exploraciones psicoanalíticas I [Psychoanalytic Explorations I]* (pp. 70–76). Buenos Aires, Argentina: Paidós.

Winnicott, D. W. (1968/1989). *The Use of an Object and Relating Through Identifications*. In C. Winnicott, R. Shepherd, & M. Davis (Eds.), *Exploraciones psicoanalíticas I [Psychoanalytic Explorations I]* (pp. 118–127). Buenos Aires, Argentina: Paidós.

Winnicott, D. W. (1971a). *Child Psychoanalytic Clinic*. Buenos Aires, Argentina: Horme.

Winnicott, D. W. (1971b). *Playing and Reality*. Barcelona, Spain: Gedisa.

Winnicott, D. W. (1977). *The Piggle: An Account of the Psychoanalytic Treatment of a Little Girl*. Barcelona, Spain: Gedisa.

Wittgenstein, L. (1973). *Tractatus Logico-Philosophicus*. Spain: Altaya.

Zaslow, S. L. (1988). Comments on "Confusion of tongues". *Contemporary Psychoanalysis*, 24, 211–224.

Zeltner, E. (2001). *Sándor Márai*. Valencia, Spain: Universitat de València.

Žižek, S. (1993). *Tarrying With the Negative: Kant, Hegel, and the Critique of Ideology*. Durham, NC: Duke University Press.

Zuleta, E. (1980). *Elogio de la dificultad [In praise of difficulty]*. In *Sobre la idealización de la vida personal y colectiva y otros ensayos* (pp. 9–14). Bogotá, Colombia: Procultura. (Original title: Elogio a la a la)

Index

For Product Safety Concerns and Information please contact our EU
representative GPSR@taylorandfrancis.com
Taylor & Francis Verlag GmbH, Kaufingerstraße 24, 80331 München, Germany

www.ingramcontent.com/pod-product-compliance
Lightning Source LLC
Chambersburg PA
CBHW050617280326
41932CB00016B/3076

9 781041 121572